# Christianity

## A SHORT INTRODUCTION

OTHER BOOKS IN THIS SERIES

*Buddhism: A Short History,* Edward Conze, ISBN 1–85168–221–X
*Buddhism: A Short Introduction,* Klaus K. Klostermaier, ISBN 1–85168–186–8
*Hinduism: A Short History,* Klaus K. Klostermaier, ISBN 1–85168–213–9
*Hindu Writings: A Short Introduction to the Major Sources,* Klaus K. Klostermaier, ISBN 1–85168–230–9
*Hinduism: A Short Introduction,* Klaus K. Klostermaier, ISBN 1–85168–220–1
*A Short Introduction to Islamic Philosophy, Theology and Mysticism,* Majid Fakhry, ISBN 1–85168–134–5
*Muhammad: A Short Biography,* Martin Forward, ISBN 1–85168–131–0
*Islam: A Short History,* William Montgomery Watt, ISBN 1–85168–205–8
*Jesus: A Short Biography,* Martin Forward, ISBN 1–85168–172–8
*Judaism: A Short History,* Lavinia and Dan Cohn-Sherbok, ISBN 1–85168–206–6
*Judaism: A Short Introduction,* Lavinia and Dan Cohn-Sherbok, ISBN 1–85168–207–4
*Judaism: A Short Reader,* Lavinia and Dan Cohn-Sherbok, ISBN 1–85168–112–4
*A Short Introduction to the Old Testament Prophets,* E. W. Heaton, ISBN 1–85168–114–0
*Sufism: A Short Introduction,* William C. Chittick, ISBN 1–85168–211–2
*The Bahá'í Faith: A Short Introduction,* Moojan Momen, ISBN 1–85168–209–0
*The Bahá'í Faith: A Short History,* Peter Smith, ISBN 1–85168–208–2

RELATED TITLES PUBLISHED BY ONEWORLD

*Resurrection Reconsidered,* Edited by Gavin D'Costa, ISBN 1–85168–113–2
*A Concise Encyclopedia of Christianity,* Geoffrey Parrinder, ISBN 1–85168–174–4
*Jesus and the Other Names: Christian Mission and Global Responsibility,* Paul F. Knitter, ISBN 1–85168–125–6
*God, Faith and the New Millennium,* Keith Ward, ISBN 1–85168–155–8
*God, Chance and Necessity,* Keith Ward, ISBN 1–85168–116–7
*In Defence of the Soul,* Keith Ward, ISBN 1–85168–040–3
*Concepts of God,* Keith Ward, ISBN 1–85168–064–0

# Christianity

## A SHORT INTRODUCTION

Keith Ward

ONEWORLD
OXFORD

# CHRISTIANITY: A SHORT INTRODUCTION

Oneworld Publications
(Sales and Editorial)
185 Banbury Road
Oxford OX2 7AR
England
http://www.oneworld-publications.com

Oneworld Publications
(US Marketing Office)
160 N Washington St.
4th Floor, Boston
MA 02114
USA

ISBN 1–85168–229–5

Cover design by Design Deluxe
Typeset by Saxon Graphics, Derby, UK
Printed and bound by Clays Ltd, St Ives plc

# CONTENTS

# 1 INTRODUCTION

A number of introductions to Christianity exist, and I have tried to think what I could say that would be an original contribution to the list. On the one hand, I want what I write to be reasonably descriptive of what actually exists, yet not just to be a factual summary. On the other hand, I want to present something of how I view Christianity, yet not just to offer a personal theological system. So in the end, I have decided to introduce Christianity by selecting some major elements of Christian belief and practice, and outlining in each case three different major types of interpretation which are held by reasonably large groups of Christians. In this way, one can get a clear idea of the diversity of the Christian world, but also of the connecting strands which enable one to identify all these very different views as Christian. Overall, what I hope a reader should get is a fair presentation of the spread of beliefs in the modern Christian world.

I am not suggesting that there are only three interpretations of each element. A threefold division is just one way of grouping types of interpretation, but of course any individual could hold views which combine different parts of different interpretations. I do myself, though I hope that from the text alone it will not be possible to infer exactly what my own beliefs are, though my general sympathies may be fairly clear.

I have tried to give as dispassionate an account of these matters as I can. Nevertheless, this is an 'insider's view' of Christian faith. I am a committed member of the Christian community, and I can hardly be expected to disguise that fact. However, this book is not meant to persuade people of the truth of Christian beliefs. I am not trying to legislate what people should believe, but some people may find that considering the various views helps them to see their own beliefs, whatever they are, in a wider context, and be aware of alternative possibilities they may have overlooked.

Christianity is the largest religion in the world, with almost two thousand million adherents. It began as a small Jewish sect in the Roman Empire, but by the fourth century it had become the official religion of the Empire. It later split, like the Empire, into the Eastern Byzantine Churches, centred on Constantinople, and the Latin Western Church, centred on Rome. It was introduced into Latin America in the sixteenth century by the Spanish, and in succeeding centuries to Asia and Africa and throughout the worldwide British Empire. Today there are Christians in every country in the world. Most European countries are 'officially' Christian. In North and South America, Russia, Australia and central and southern Africa, the majority religion is Christian. Only in a geographical belt running from North Africa through Arabia and India to China, South East Asia and Japan, have Christians failed to establish a dominant position. There, they co-exist with varying degrees of friendship or mutual suspicion with adherents of Islam, Hinduism, Buddhism and other Indian- or Asian-based faiths.

Like all religions, Christianity in the developed world exists in a largely secular context, though the anti-religious invective of State Communism in Russia and China has now virtually collapsed. Christianity naturally looks very different in the differing cultures in which it exists. The Roman Catholic Church is by far the largest, with over a thousand million members. Though it has a very centralised government in the Vatican, in Rome, it is in practice very diverse. There are very traditional Catholics, who wish to see a hierarchical, politically conservative church, with a carefully defined dogmatic faith, to be accepted on the authority of the Pope. There are very radical Catholics, who ally themselves with those who fight for liberation from perceived political and economic oppression in Latin America, and who may take the view that the Vatican is a long way away and in a different culture. There are Catholics who oppose the alleged rationalism and humanism of the secular world, as enemies of faith, and there are Catholics who embrace the European Enlightenment as liberating faith from outmoded forms of thought. So, while it is possible to say what the official attitude of the Vatican is, it is much more difficult to make any accurate generalisations about what Catholics throughout the world actually believe.

The *World Christian Encyclopedia* estimates that there are about 373 million Protestants in the world. They belong to a number of different denominations (Presbyterian, Methodist, Baptist and so forth), but generally accept non-hierarchical and decentralised forms of church government, and stress personal faith in Jesus Christ more than membership of a particular institutional church. In this century many of these denominations have united into larger confederations, like the Church of South India, formed in 1947 by a union of Anglican, Methodist and Presbyterian churches. Some, however, insist on the right to form independent congregations of disciples of Christ, though they may cultivate friendly relations with other churches. Protestants are very active in missionary work throughout the world, and churches are expanding rapidly in Africa and Latin America. The World Council of Churches, formed in 1948, is a general co-ordinating body to which most Protestant churches are affiliated.

There are about 170 million Eastern Orthodox Christians, who historically originated in the Eastern (Byzantine) Roman Empire, and have always retained a loyalty to the sort of Greek theology current in the first centuries of Christian expansion. They are organised as national churches, under their own bishops, and acknowledging allegiance to the Patriarch of Constantinople. They do not acknowledge the authority of the Roman Pope, as Catholics understand it, though they usually grant him a primacy of honour. Orthodox Christians have a very distinctive form of worship, which is usually very traditional, and a high regard for the monastic life. They are found mostly in the Greek-influenced countries of Eastern Europe and in Russia, though their emphasis on mystical theology and on the beauty of the liturgy has led to a modest growth in other parts of the world.

There are many other Christians, like the worldwide Anglican communion of national Episcopal churches, the non-Orthodox 'Church of the East', and many indigenous churches, which do not fit neatly into this categorisation. The world of Christianity is a large, plural and ever-changing one, and even these denominations should not be assumed to be final in their present form. In an increasingly interdependent world, where global communication is instant and travel is easy, churches cannot remain isolated in local cultural enclaves. One major challenge all churches face in the third Christian millennium is how the very diverse cultures of the world can be both validated and transformed by Christianity, and how Christianity should be transformed by its embrace of or relationship to these cultures.

It is no longer true that Christianity is European or Western, even though historically it has been associated with European expansion and colonialisation. How will the cultures of Africa and Latin America change Christian perceptions, as the cultures of ancient Greece and of Renaissance Europe changed them in the past? How can Christianity relate in a positive and mutually enhancing way to those ancient cultures which have mostly resisted its influence, the cultures of Arabia, India, China, Japan and South East Asia?

Christianity, which is now completely international, is still greatly influenced by its European past. But it is in Europe that faith seems weakest, and in the developing world that it is at its most vital. So Christianity may look for its future to the non-Western world, and the new insights it can bring to complement old traditions. It is unlikely that the whole world will become completely Christian, though Christians will be able to give an international dimension to social action wherever they exist. Christians have the opportunity to use their influence for greater human flourishing and world justice, as members of a major global organisation which is overtly dedicated to striving for a community of justice and peace, and for care for the oppressed. To do this effectively, the churches have to work out how best to overcome the distrust they have sometimes had for one another, and learn how best to serve God's world in love. And they have to learn to relate positively and helpfully to those who do not adhere to the same beliefs, but who have a commitment to social justice, and who may be able to offer complementary insights into the nature and purposes of God.

One challenge to modern Christianity is to become a truly global but non-imperialist faith, in constructive dialogue both with other sorts of Christians, and with those of other world views. Another is to re-orient itself to the scientific revolution which has transformed the world since the sixteenth century. Like people in general, Christians may take many attitudes to modern scientific advances – perhaps welcoming the amazing advances in medical care, while fearing the equally amazing advances in developing weapons of destruction and techniques of genetic manipulation. Changes in economics and technology have freed women from economic dependency and an imposed vocation of child-bearing, so that new questions of achieving true human equality, in the light of the obvious male dominance of past centuries, need to be faced. Similarly, new scientific awareness of the fragility of our planetary eco-system and of the interdependency of all things in that system, necessitates fresh ethical thinking on how to sustain the earth as a habitation for living beings.

Traditional faiths did not have to face these questions in this form. Yet Christianity, in common with many other faiths, has a commitment to human justice, to reconciliation with and compassion for friends and enemies alike, and to caring for the earth as God's creation and gift to humanity. In this rapidly changing world, the churches will have to change too, to think out a new vision of God's creation in the vastly expanded cosmic context of modern science, and in view of the quite new human ability to change the earth itself.

The Christian tradition has two thousand years of reflection and prayer to help it in this task. But it could be that it is as yet only at the beginning of learning to fulfil its true vocation of helping to transform the earth to become a place where the spirit of love can bring many different sorts of human communities to a mutually enriching fulfilment.

This is a personal view of the main challenges facing Christianity in the modern world, though it aims to be based on a reasonably impartial view of the Christian churches as they actually exist. These churches, however, may sometimes be so far apart in beliefs and practices that they may seem like different religions. There are nevertheless central beliefs that unite them. One is a basic belief that the universe has been created by an immensely wise and powerful being. The universe thus has a purpose for its existence, it is not just an accident. This purpose has been made known on the planet earth in and through the life and teaching of Jesus of Nazareth, and the purpose can ultimately be achieved by human beings who follow that life and teaching.

Beyond these basic beliefs, there is a huge variety of other beliefs and practices, some of them seemingly in sharp conflict with others. In the following pages I will try to outline some of the major Christian schools of thought.

# 2 CREATION

All Christians believe that God created the universe. This is probably the most important of all Christian beliefs, because almost everything else will depend on how people understand the nature of God as creator. Even on the subject of creation there are different views, but almost all Christians believe that the universe is not self-existent, but has been intentionally brought into being (created) by a being beyond it, which *is* self-existent. Most scientists today think that the universe is between 10 and 20 thousand million years old, and that it has expanded from a primeval dot of virtually infinite density and mass to its present complex state, consisting of millions of galaxies, themselves containing millions of stars, and millions of planets. On most scientific accounts, the universe will go on expanding and cooling at the same time, until it runs out of heat and comes to a frozen stand-still. Or it may collapse in on itself again, and all things will end in an inescapable blaze of intense cosmic radiation. Whatever exactly happens, it seems clear that this physical universe will one day, a very long time in the future, cease to exist in anything like its present form. The universe, in other words, has a beginning and an end, at both of which nothing much happens. All the interesting things happen in the middle of its history.

Another thing most scientists agree about is that the universe is not chaotic. On the contrary, it seems to work in accordance with fairly simple principles which are elegant and beautiful, mathematically speaking. It is an extremely complex, mathematically elegant totality. Moreover, by the working of the laws of physics it has produced out of itself beings which are able to understand their own nature. In human beings – and maybe in countless other forms of conscious life on other planets, unknown to us – the universe becomes self-conscious. Almost inconceivably complex bundles of atoms and molecules generate the amazing capacity to know and marvel at their own nature, and even to change it. The universe is not only beautiful; it is capable of knowing that it is, of admiring that beauty, and of creating new forms of beauty out of itself.

So the universe grows from an elementally simple state, where there is no knowledge, no complexity, no freedom and no creativity. It becomes conscious, at least in the most complex physical states known to us, human brains, and produces beings who are creative and free, who understand, communicate, love and create. Eventually it dies, probably returning to a frozen immobility where time itself ceases to have meaning, since there will be no change by which to measure it.

Perhaps that is all there is – an amazing, awe-inspiring story, which has no further explanation. But most people feel that the story suggests something else – such beauty, complexity, intelligibility and consciousness of value suggest a master consciousness which has brought it into being precisely because of the value it expresses. A cosmic mind could indeed produce such a universe, which realises sorts of values which could otherwise not exist at all. The creator could enjoy those values, and could also have the purpose of creating other personal agents who could enjoy them as well. Thus this vast cosmos could very easily be seen as being the purposive product of an immensely wise and powerful mind. That mind is the creator, causing the universe to exist for the sake of its beauty and value. On this view, the scientific story is one that fits very well with the Christian belief in creation.

## FIRST VIEW: SIX-DAY CREATION

Despite the majesty and persuasiveness of the scientific story, some Christians feel committed to a fairly literal interpretation of the Bible, according to which (in Genesis chapter 1) the creator brings humans into being in a six-day process, beginning with the creation of light, then atmosphere, then the life-bearing earth, sun, moon and stars, birds and fish, and finally animals and human beings. Any such literal account does have problems with many of the claims made by contemporary science. It also seems in tension with another creation account given in Genesis chapter 2, where things appear to happen in a different order (humans exist before the animals, for example). And it concentrates on the planet earth as the centre of the universe, relegating the stars to a subordinate position. So it is a difficult view to maintain today. Nevertheless the account can be defended with some subtlety (for instance, by confining the account to events seen from the perspective of the earth, or by interpreting 'days' as long periods of time), and it needs to be assessed on its merits. Its central point is that the universe has a creator, who brings it into being by a gradual temporal process (the six 'days'). The process culminates in beings who are capable of conscious relationship to the creator, and whose task it is to care for and shape the earth and its other living forms. Despite the fact that it conflicts seriously with most scientific accounts, the core of the literalist view is that there is a creator with a purpose which is gradually worked out in the universe, and in which humans have an important role to play. That, I think, is the important spiritual teaching of the Biblical creation stories. Whether or not they are to be interpreted literally will largely depend on how one judges the available evidence from the natural sciences.

## SECOND VIEW: TIMELESS CREATION

Most Christians accept that contemporary science gives an accurate history of the universe. The two Genesis stories are then not taken literally, but are seen as poetic accounts with a spiritual teaching of the dependence of all things on God. As a matter of fact, the best known Christian theologians have always stressed that the important point of the stories is not the literal account of what happened when the universe began. The stories present in the form of a narrative a teaching which is really about the present relationship of human beings, and of the whole universe in which they exist, to God.

St Augustine put this very clearly, in his classic work, 'The City of God', written in a Roman province of North Africa in the early fifth century. He pointed out that if God is really the creator of the whole universe, then God is the creator of space and time, as well as of everything in space–time. But then Augustine poses the question: if God creates time, what was God doing before he created time? The catch is that, if God created time itself, there cannot have been anything before time, and so God cannot have been doing anything at all!

This may sound like a trick – as though we have been trapped into agreeing that God could not have existed before the universe, or could not have thought about what he was doing before he did it. But it actually makes a very profound point, which Augustine brings out very clearly. What it shows, says Augustine, is that God is not in time at all. God, as the creator of time, is beyond the limitations of time. God exists 'eternally' – that is, not in time as we understand it at all. It is from that timeless eternity that God creates the whole space–time universe.

Thus Augustine forces us to think of the creation in a more sophisticated way. It is not that first of all God was alone and wondered what to do. Then, at a certain time, he decided to create a universe, so that the creation is the beginning of the universe – which is what a literal interpretation of the Genesis stories may lead us to think. What we have to try to grasp is that the creation is a relation between eternity and time, between the eternal God and the whole spatio-temporal universe. We might say that the whole of time issues from the eternity of God in one intelligent and purposeful act. The creation is not the beginning of the universe. It is the dependence of the whole universe, from beginning to end, and at every point in the middle, on one intelligent, eternal and self-existent being, God.

The temporal form of the Genesis stories might hide that fact from us, making us think that the creation was just God getting the universe going, and then, perhaps, having a rest. What we have to see is that every moment of time is dependent on the eternal God, who is beyond every time (not 'before' or 'after' time!).

Once we see this, we can also see that it does not matter exactly what happened in the first few days of the existence of the universe. It does not matter if the universe never had a beginning at all. Scientists do think that the universe began, at the moment of the 'Big Bang'. But the Christian doctrine of creation is not concerned with whether the universe began or not. It just wants to say that, whether time began or whether it has always existed, it depends for its existence on an eternal being, a being beyond the limitations of time. That being is God, and we understand something very important about God when we realise that God is eternal.

One of the important things we realise is that God is quite beyond our imaginations. We can only imagine things that exist in time. So, when we try to imagine God, we naturally imagine him as thinking, deciding and acting in time. The Bible often speaks of God in this way – even as 'walking in the Garden of Eden' (Genesis 3:8), or changing his mind from time to time. We do not want to say that these things are totally false. But once we really grasp the doctrine of creation, we see that they can only be pictures to help us to think of God, but they do not really tell us what God is like. Such pictures may be revealed by God, to help us to relate ourselves to God in an appropriate way. But things go badly wrong when we think God is literally like those pictures, however helpful they might be. For the eternal God is wholly beyond our imaginations, infinitely bigger and more mysterious than we can ever think.

That is partly why the Bible forbids making any images of God (Exodus 20:4), and why the 'Holy of Holies', the innermost secret sanctuary of the Jewish Temple, had no image of God in it. God is beyond all the limitations of our thoughts, and we must never try to reduce God to something that we can see or feel. So a very important part of the Christian doctrine of creation is that it insists on a very radical distinction between God and the whole of the universe. The universe begins and ends. It changes and develops. It could easily have been very different, as far as we can see. But it could not exist at all if it did not depend on a very different reality, the eternal reality of God. God does not begin or end, but exists eternally. God does not grow or decay, but is one and unchanging. God is, in a way we cannot fully understand, self-existent – does not depend on anything else for existence, but is, as the medieval philosopher Boethius put it, 'the unlimited ocean of being'.

It is quite inadequate, therefore, to think of God as finite, or as being a person who is something like a human person. God is the ultimate self-existent mystery of being, and the whole universe exists just because God brings it into existence by one intelligent and intentional act. All pictures of God, even those in the Bible, must only be aids to our imagination, since God is radically different from anything we can imagine. At this point, some Christians may feel a little uneasy. Have we not a true picture of God in the person of Jesus, after all? Do Christians not say that Jesus is God? So God must be imaginable, at least in the form of Jesus.

I will be saying more about this when we come to think about the doctrine of the Incarnation in chapter 6, about the way in which God is known in Jesus. But for the moment it may be helpful to hold a picture in our minds. Think of the whole universe, from beginning to end, from the Big Bang to the Big Freeze, as produced in one act by the eternal God. That is basically Augustine's picture of creation. All the things in the universe are finite, and naturally you cannot squeeze the infinite God into a finite universe. So God will always be infinitely greater than the universe, and radically different from it. Yet at the same time, the universe will in a way express what God is, in something like the way in which a painting might express something of the personality of the painter. Some paintings might be better expressions of that personality than others. So, in the universe, some parts of it may express the nature of God better than others. It might be possible for a particular part of the universe to express the nature of God, in a way suitable for finite beings to understand, in a uniquely clear or adequate way. Christians would say that the person of Jesus expresses the nature of God in such a uniquely adequate way.

So a Christian would want to say that Jesus gives an adequate picture of the nature of God. But that means that this is the best picture which humans can understand. This is what God is like, insofar as God is expressed in time. The Christian claim is that the eternal God can express himself in time – again, just as a painter might express himself in a particular painting. But God will also remain far beyond time, just as the painter will remain distinct from his painting.

Now of course the analogy of the painter is not adequate to what Christians want to say about Jesus. For Jesus is a living, active person, not just a painting. In some way, this living person is a true image in time of a God who is beyond time. He is the temporal expression of an eternal God. Perhaps what it comes down to is this: Christians would say that there can be finite images of the eternal God, and Jesus is the perfect image of God. But we still must never confuse the image, the temporal expression, with the eternal reality, as if we were reducing the eternal into time, without remainder. There is a true expression of God in time, and so a true image. But it is still an image, and not the total reality of God.

The important thing, then, is to realise that all images, even Jesus, must be treated as images of the eternal God, not as reductions of God to some finite thing. Reducing God to any finite thing would be idolatry. But seeing a finite thing as an image of God, or a medium through which one can see God, or a vehicle of God's purposes, is not idolatry at all. Indeed, Christians would probably say that you have to have such finite images to help to relate to the eternal God. As long as you remember that you are never reducing the eternal to something less, you can worship the eternal God in the person of Jesus, who is the way God appears in time.

The doctrine of creation, then, does not wholly exclude God from time. But it reminds us that God is infinitely far beyond time, even if he can truly appear in time. As God is beyond time, the future is as present to God as the present or the past. We experience our lives as passing through a series of times, one after the other, but to God the whole of created being exists in one timeless eternal 'now'. God sees what is future to us as eternally present. So God decrees what is to happen in the whole of the universe in his one eternal act of creation. That is basically what Augustine means by 'predestination'. It is as if God creates the whole of our lives at once, and so knows and decrees exactly what is going to happen to us at every moment of our lives. The future never slips from God's control, and all things are under the hand of God.

## THIRD VIEW: CONTINUOUS CREATION

Such a view of creation, however, has a price. The price is that God can never do anything new, that he has not eternally decided. Humans can never do anything that God has not, in some sense, eternally ordained that they should do. And God can never respond to human acts in new, creative ways, which are not already fixed by eternal and changeless decree. So some Christians, accepting that God is continuously creating, as the classical view holds, add that at each moment God is free to create in ways which he had not previously decided. God can, for instance, call Moses to serve him, and then wait to see how Moses will respond. In view of the nature of Moses' response, God can then shape the future in an appropriate way. Creation will be a sort of continuing conversation between God and created persons, in which what happens will always depend partly on what creatures decide – though in the end, God remains in control.

This view of creation places much more stress on the reality of time, and it even makes God temporal, in that even God has an open future, makes new decisions, and changes in response to what human beings and other creatures do. Christians who hold the second view might object that this subjects God to the limitation of time, and so is unsatisfactory. If God is in time, he cannot be completely in control of the future, and cannot be the creator of time, which seems to exist independently of God.

Those who hold the third view, however, can agree that God exists beyond the limitations of time. But they would stress that the mode of such eternal existence is beyond human understanding, and that we have no access to the inner life of God. Certainly, God cannot be limited by time, as some sort of independent reality. But even those who hold the second view accept that the eternal God can truly appear or express the divine nature in time – that is what the Incarnation claims. So why can we not say that God freely chooses to enter into time, to become temporal, precisely as one expression of the unlimited reality of God?

Many contemporary theologians – like the Swiss Reformed theologian Karl Barth – would argue that God is free to become temporal. While remaining beyond time, God can also have a freely willed temporal expression. But if God is truly temporal, then he can enter into a real relationship with finite persons. He can leave them free to make their own decisions, respond to those decisions, and co-operate with them in helping them to avoid evil and choose virtue.

If you take this view, you will not think of God creating the whole universe, from the first moment to the last, in one eternal act. Rather, you will think of God creating the universe in a series of acts, one after the other. So he might create Abraham, and call him to leave Ur and seek a new place to live. He might then wait to see how Abraham responds, before he creates the next bit of the universe, which will take Abraham's response into account. If Abraham had refused to leave Ur, the divine plan for the earth would have taken a different shape. But Abraham said yes, so the divine promise of a covenant with his descendants was made.

This gives human freedom and human decision-making a very important part to play in the working out of the divine plan for this earth. Some people fear that it puts the divine plan too much at risk, and makes God virtually powerless in his own universe. However, those who hold the third view would usually insist that God retains the power to do whatever he wants, and in particular to make sure that his purposes succeed eventually. But he restrains that power so that humans can be free and responsible. God gives humans a strictly limited freedom. They can thwart God's plans to quite a great extent – causing conflict and suffering and disharmony – but in the end God will realise his purpose for creation.

What that means is that God will not be able to predict exactly what is going to happen in the history of this planet, for example. He does not make Abraham decide in one way rather than another, and so he does not know in advance exactly what Abraham will decide. But God does plan to bring humans to salvation – to full knowledge and love of God. So he will ensure that happens, in one way or another. The failure of one plan leads to the forming of another, and God will go on devising new plans until one of them succeeds. However many failures there are along the way, in the end the general plan will succeed, because God has the patience, wisdom and power to ensure that it does.

This is a much more interactive view of creation, which sees God as co-operating with finite persons, and giving them real responsibility to realise the divine plan for creation. It makes predestination much more difficult than on the second view. Indeed, on the third view God does not predestine in one eternal decree everything that is going to happen in history. But we can still say that God predestines that many will come to salvation, even though he might not be able to say in advance who exactly they are (some theologians, like Karl Barth, hold out the possibility that God might actually predestine everyone to salvation, and then of course he would know who they were).

God's interaction with creation can only take full effect when there exist responsible moral agents in the universe with whom God can interact. But this view does have some implications for our understanding of the physical structure of the universe. If the physical universe existed for billions of years before any created persons came into being, then God could be thought of as preparing the universe to be a suitable home for personal beings – for example, building into its fundamental laws elements of flexibility and 'randomness' which will allow creaturely freedom to come into existence in due course. It will be a probabilistic universe, rather than a deterministic one. Yet the universe will remain a place of elegant and intelligible beauty, expressing the wisdom and beauty of God even as it moves towards the emergence of those created persons whose destiny it is to become co-creators with God of the future.

On this view, God is continuously creating the universe, taking into account the free decisions of any rational creatures in the universe, and shaping an open future in co-operation with them. Finally, however, God controls the process, and will either eliminate those elements which remain resistant to him, or shape finite beings into freely responsive channels of his creative wisdom and love. Thus the universe is a creative and co-operative adventure of a God who is himself, at least in one important aspect of his being, in time – itself seen as the condition of real creativity.

# 3 THE EXISTENCE OF EVIL

To believe in creation is to believe that the universe is brought into being by an immensely wise and powerful God, who creates it in order to realise specific values which could only exist in a universe like this. To some people, however, the universe seems to contain too much accident and cruelty to be the creation of a cosmic mind who wants to create a worthwhile universe. The problem of randomness and suffering is a major problem for any theist. But this is a point at which discoveries in modern science can help Christian reflection.

The scientific view shows the universe to have great beauty and rationality, which underlies even apparently chaotic events. What may seem random at first sight in fact turns out to be the product of exquisitely interwoven forces at the sub-atomic level. So-called 'chaos theory' shows how events that seem to have no pattern in fact result from extremely elegant and highly ordered forces at a deeper level. In that sense, at least, the universe really is beautiful and therefore good in a sort of aesthetic sense.

Many contemporary scientists also point out that there is a high degree of necessity about the universe. It is not just a collection of events which happen to be related to one another. The fundamental forces of nature – the forces of gravity, electro-magnetism and so on – need to be exactly what they are to give rise to a universe with conscious living beings in it. The laws of nature need to proceed just as they do if such beings are to be truly parts of an evolving, emergent universe. Conflict and destruction are as necessary to such a universe as are co-operation and creative emergence, and indeed one cannot exist without the other. God could not create such a universe without the suffering which results from such conflict. Even so, one might think that the creator of this universe, if there is one, does not seem to have very much concern with suffering and pain.

The creator of a universe as immense as this would be no quasi-human mind, writ large. Christian theologians are agreed that, even though God can appear in time in the form of the human person of Jesus, it would be quite wrong to think of God the creator as anything like a human being. But it would be right to speak of God as conscious, as having immense power and wisdom, and even as enjoying the values that finite minds see and enjoy only in a tiny part. God is a reality of consciousness, wisdom, power and bliss, and the whole story of our universe is perhaps only the smallest transient moment in the creative activity of God. But can this amazing creator really be called 'good'? Christians do think the creator is good, though mainly in the sense that any being of wisdom, power and bliss, who creates things as a form of self-expression and in order to enjoy them, is 'good', because its own existence is desirable. That is certainly one thing the word 'good' means. A thing is good if it is desirable for its own sake. God, being wise, powerful, beautiful and happy, is certainly something which it is worth having just for its own sake, and so is supremely desirable. In that sense, at least, it is right to call the creator good.

But how can suffering and evil exist in a universe created by a good (desirable) God, who wants to enjoy its goodness? Before one can answer that question, one must first answer another question which is almost irresistible: if such a God caused the universe, what caused God? The idea of God was formed partly because the physical universe was seen not to be self-existent. It was seen to come into being and pass away, to have no seeming necessity in itself, but to consist just of things each of which depends upon other things, without any finally stable stopping point. God, however, is a reality which does not come into being or pass away, does not depend on anything other than itself, and does not derive its existence from anything else at all. God exists necessarily – there is just no alternative to the existence of God, for God is the principle of being itself, without which no beings would be possible at all.

This may seem a very abstract idea. But in fact it can make a real difference to the way a Christian experiences the world. For what is needed to see the real character of belief in God is a sort of spiritual sensibility, a sense of infinity known in and through the finite, a sense of finite things as images of infinite being, however partial or corrupted they sometimes are. It is not some abstract philosophical argument which gets to a 'First Cause' of the universe. It is what the early nineteenth-century Prussian theologian Friedrich Schleiermacher called 'a sense and taste for the infinite' which leads one to apprehend the stable, unchanging, unlimitedly actual being which underlies every part of the finite universe we know.

So God is not in any physical form, not in the space and time of this universe at all. Nor is God the being who starts the universe going, and then retires behind the scenes. Rather, God is the unlimited consciousness which holds the universe in being at every moment, from its beginning to its end, and perhaps holds countless other universes in being as well. Such a God is more immense than the human mind can imagine. One could certainly not come across God, as one might come across a stone in a field. But we can think of God as a uniquely self-existent being, more like mind or consciousness than like anything else, which wills the universe into existence for the sake of its goodness, its beauty and perfection.

Perhaps one might see the universe as a vast work of art, gradually unfolding all the themes implicit in its first beginning, under the hands of a master creator. For a believer in God, one of the most rewarding human experiences might be a sense of communion with the mind of the creator through the beauty of his works. To cultivate such a sense of communion is, I think, one of the main points of prayer. For after all, the highest form of prayer is not asking for things, or even thanking God for the many good and beautiful things we experience. It is worship, and worship is the contemplation of what is supremely worthwhile for its own sake.

You may admire a beautiful sunset for its own sake. But to learn to admire the mind which expresses only the smallest part of its creativity in such a sunset, but which does truly express itself in it, is like moving from a world of shadows into a world of light, in which the reality which casts those shadows can begin to be seen in its true nature. So Plato said, at least, and Plato's thought has from the beginning been one of the chief sources of Christian thinking about God.

Plato did not really think of God as a creator, but more as an architect or designer. But the great Christian theologian Augustine took Plato's ideas of the designer and of the world of Forms (the pattern of God's designs) and of the half-real world of time and space, and united them by placing the Forms in the mind of God, and seeing time and space themselves as created by God, not as somehow separately existing. Modern physics supports this unification, when it sees space–time as finite, and thus as capable of being brought into being and destroyed. The mind of the creator alone is indestructible, and it is the guarantee of the order and stability of the cosmos.

Now we are in a position to see one way of tackling the question of the existence of suffering in creation. God is not a being who just happens to be the way God is, as though God might have been quite different, or might change in essential nature at any time. God is self-existent and immutable, beyond time and space, the one and only source of all other existing things, the principle of being itself. If that is so, there is no point asking why God is not any better than God is. God could not be better – or worse – than God is, for God's being is the immutable foundation of every other being there could ever be.

I have suggested that God is good, in being supremely desirable, both to himself and to all beings who see him properly. God is also good, because God creates the universe in order to realise some very good things that would not otherwise have existed. Moreover, God might be good inasmuch as he wants all created persons to have the chance of eternal happiness – that is something Christian revelation claims. God might be good in all these ways, even though the universe that God creates will necessarily contain evil and suffering, which even God cannot prevent. We do not know why not, since we do not know the inner being of God. But we can see that it might well be true that, if God cannot be any other than God is in the essential divine nature, then even God might not be able to prevent certain evils which seem to arise as the shadow-side of the good things that the created universe makes possible.

Medieval theologians put this by saying that evil is the privation of good. They did not mean that evil does not exist at all. They meant that it is an absence of good, something parasitic on good, though perhaps a necessary side-effect of good. A relatively trivial example would be the way in which the immensely worthwhile experience of playing the violin beautifully has, as a necessary side-effect, years of hard, boring and sometimes painful practising. It does indeed seem obvious that some goods – like the attaining of many human excellences – do involve painful and disliked events. So we can see how some evil could be involved in a universe created by a good God.

The problem remains – does this universe not contain just too much evil for that? There are serious problems about assessing just how much evil would be too much, once we have admitted that some evil at least is permissible. Obviously, Christians believe that a good God does create a universe like this, so there cannot be too much evil. But the sheer amount and horror of suffering, at Auschwitz, or in Vietnam, or Leningrad or in the trenches of Flanders, might make the firmest believer waver at times.

## FIRST VIEW: THE PRIVATION OF BEING

Christians have developed three main sorts of responses to such serious doubts. One is associated with the thirteenth-century theologian Thomas Aquinas. It insists that the creator is far beyond the possibility of moral assessment by human beings. The creator's will is absolute, and no creature can understand why it is as it is. God is still supremely desirable, and it is right to worship God without requiring an answer to questions about God's reasons for creating. God will bring good out of evil, but that evil is somehow rooted in the ultimate being of God itself – not as something positive, but as a sort of shadow of nothingness involved in creation, a privation of being which belongs to creation. It is just necessarily there, and there is no point in wishing it away. This tradition is nevertheless clear and insistent that suffering should be eliminated whenever it is possible to do so – it is not to be thought of as good, in any sense. A robust statement of this view would be that God creates weal and woe, light and darkness (Isaiah 45:7), but God wills that good should triumph, and that we should fight evil by uniting ourselves to God's positive will for the triumph of good.

## SECOND VIEW: THE AUTONOMY OF MATTER

Another response is to say that God is limited by the nature of matter. Perhaps matter exists, as Plato thought, as a material which God shapes towards goodness, though God can never control it completely. Some scholars think that the second verse of the very first chapter of Genesis assumes that there is a 'great deep', a sort of primeval chaos, out of which God shapes the heaven and earth. Process theologians, following the thought of the twentieth-century philosopher A.N. Whitehead, stress that all created things must have their own autonomy to some extent, so even God cannot control them totally. There are elements of chaos or of freedom in any finite cosmos which even God cannot simply eliminate. God is the most powerful being, but even such a being cannot simply control the wills of all the finite beings that exist. God must seek to persuade or influence, rather than completely control. This response is like the first one, in holding that it is metaphysically impossible for God to eliminate all evil. But it is unlike the first, in claiming that all finite agents have a certain self-determining freedom, which even God cannot infringe or direct.

## THIRD VIEW: THE MISUSE OF FREEDOM

A third response, partly held by Augustine, but found in its full form in twentieth-century theologians like John Hick, is to say that most of the worst suffering is the result of the free choice of creatures to reject God and choose egoism. On this view, there *is* far more evil in the universe than there need or should have been. Something has gone wrong somewhere, which needs to be put right. God could perhaps have controlled creatures totally, but then they could never have become persons, with responsibility and freedom. God gave at least some creatures the possibility of freedom, but did not want them to choose the evil they have in fact chosen. So God had to create a universe which would make such freedom able to develop – and perhaps that had to be a not fully determined or completely perfect universe, so that created persons can have the possibility of shaping their world towards perfection (or away from it) themselves.

Some Christians think that God created spiritual beings – angels – some of which chose to put themselves before God. Under their leader, Satan, these 'fallen angels' control parts of creation, and are responsible for many of its destructive aspects. Other Christians, however, regard talk of Satan as a metaphor for those propensities to egoism and pride which are built into the nature of emergent persons, and become constant temptations to evil in the lives of human beings (see chapter 5).

Like the second view, this response emphasises the reality and importance of radical freedom to disobey God's will. Perhaps such freedom is necessary if there is to be any possibility of a relationship of freely self-giving love between beings. So freedom might be a condition of there being a true moral community in the universe. But the third response gives God the final sovereignty, so that the divine plan can be guaranteed to succeed in the end. God is not doomed to be always trying to persuade, without any guarantee of success. Freedom is given so that a moral community can come into being. But when it does, God can perfect it, or finally eliminate those who refuse to be members of it.

All these views seek to show that the existence of evil and suffering in the universe is compatible with the existence of a good creator, and that we can get some hint of how even the most powerful possible being could not wholly eliminate all suffering. In some sense there are necessities in the nature of being itself which make evil ineliminable from a created universe like this. But none of these views claim that we can understand the necessities of the divine nature, or that we can actually explain why every sort of evil exists. Like Job, in the Bible, all believers in God will finally bow before the utter mystery of the divine being, from which all things arise, and to which all things must finally return (Job 42:1–6). But it is possible rationally to believe that the creator is a supremely desirable being, whom creatures can come to know and love, and whose desire that good should finally triumph will in the end be realised. Christians will insist that, wherever suffering exists and can be eliminated, it should be. And they will accept that a very great deal of suffering on this planet earth is due to the immoral choices of generations of human beings, who have misused their God-given freedom. In the human world, at least, the purposes of God have been opposed by the very persons whom God created in order that they might co-operate in realising God's intentions for this cosmos. Christianity begins from a perception that there is something wrong with the way the world is, and that the responsibility for this falls very largely on human beings.

# 4 THE SOUL

Human beings are certainly not the centre of the universe, which is a vast cosmos of a billion galaxies and billions of stars. We exist on a small blue planet at the edge of a rather modest galaxy. Nevertheless, the human brain is the single most complex object we have ever come across, and in human beings there has come to exist the extraordinary capacity to be aware of and to comprehend the structure of the universe of which we are part. Atheists might see human consciousness as a by-product of a blind process of billions of random atomic accidents. But it is equally reasonable to see the whole cosmic process as purposively directed towards the existence of conscious, rational, moral agents. Beginning with the unconscious simplicity of a point of infinite density and mass, the cosmos exploded into being, not as a chaotic and unstructured jumble, but – amazingly – into a process which assembled highly patterned, elegantly ordered and increasingly complex structures. The fundamental forces of gravity, electro-magnetism and nuclear energy reacted and integrated in such a way that relatively enduring atomic elements of hydrogen and helium formed. They in turn, through nuclear reactions at the heart of exploding stars, built more complex atoms like carbon, which were to prove capable of forming the large self-replicating molecules of which life is made up. Those molecules in turn built the even more complex and integrated structures of organic bodies, which could reproduce and mutate to build up ever more responsive life-forms, with central nervous systems enabling them to develop in ways suited to their environment. Further complexity, specialisation and adaptation led to the formation in some of these life-forms of the brain, and then to the development of the unique neo-cortex of *homo sapiens sapiens*. So at the end (so far) of that long process of increasing complexity and order, organisms came into existence which could be aware, could reason and speculate about their own existence, could make moral choices, and even begin to change and control their own habitat.

It is, I think, very hard not to see this as a purposive process, a process designed from the first to produce moral and rational consciousnesses. Such consciousnesses may exist in many parts of the universe, and they may take many different physical forms. But we only know of them on this planet, in the form of human beings. However much we may regard non-human animals as having a deep affinity with human animals, it is a fact that no other animal on earth debates about and decides upon moral and social policies, discovers and hands on to its successors precise information about the structure of the universe, and creates structured forms of sound and vision (music and art) which are encoded physically to be enjoyed by future generations. Human beings may be evolved, like all other life-forms, from the most primitive one-celled forms of organic life, but they are truly unique on earth in their possession of the capacity for abstract conceptual thought, imaginative creativity and responsible moral agency.

For Christians, the uniqueness of human life is marked by saying that humans are made 'in the image of God' (Genesis 1:26). They are formed out of dust – we now know, quite literally out of stardust. They are genuine parts of the material universe. But in their understanding, creativity and freedom they reflect in a special way the nature of the creator who set the whole process spinning on its way, and who holds it on its appointed course.

The belief that humans are created in the image of God does not mean that they look like God. It means that their unique capacities to understand, to create and to act in freedom reflect the nature of the God who is supreme wisdom, creativity and freedom. From the Christian point of view, human wisdom, creativity and freedom are never total. Being creatures of God, the highest human understanding is to share in the divine wisdom, the highest human creativity is to share in the divine beauty, and the highest human freedom is to share in the divine love. Human persons find their fulfilment, not in being wholly autonomous or self-governing, but in being participants in, finite images of, the divine wisdom, beauty and love. To be made in the image of God is not only to be something like God; it is to be a sharer in the nature of God.

The traditional way of marking the uniqueness of human beings is to speak of 'the soul', but that is a much misunderstood idea, so much so that it may be better simply to talk about 'the person' instead. Nevertheless, there are a number of ways of thinking about the soul in Christian tradition, though most thoughtful Christians would admit that probably none of them gives a completely adequate account of what the distinctive nature of human existence is.

## FIRST VIEW: DUALISM OF SOUL AND BODY

Some Christians think that the human capacities of intellectual understanding, creative imagination and moral freedom are essentially spiritual, or non-material. The thoughts, images and decisions of the mind are not in space, and they are not made out of matter. God is not in space, has no material body, yet understands, creates and decides. So, it may be thought, the human soul is not in space. It is the core of the human person, and when it understands, imagines and makes free moral decisions, these activities are not determined by physical events which happen in the brain.

Of course the brain and the soul are very closely bound together. The human soul is embodied in the material world. Its sensory images and feelings are caused by events in the physical world, and immediately by events in the brain. What the soul can think, feel and do is limited by the state of its brain and body. Yet despite this close connection, the soul has an area of free activity which is not simply determined by laws of physical causality in the brain. Events in the brain will affect what the soul understands and feels. But the reactions and responses of the soul will in turn affect what happens in the brain. If someone pricks me with a pin, my soul will feel pain. My reaction is partly governed by my own free response, so that I can by an act of will restrain the natural tendency of the body to pull away.

On this view, each soul is one continuing spiritual individual, which is conscious, understands, feels and decides. It comes into existence at a specific time (usually thought to be at some undetermined time between physical conception and birth), and it then continues to exist in close causal connection with a particular physical body. After the death of the body, it may continue to exist. Indeed, Augustine held that the soul is by nature incorruptible. It can be destroyed by God, but it is by nature immortal, and will continue to exist unless God destroys it. Souls may exist without bodies – though they will need to have some way of obtaining information and to have some means of acting, if they are to have reasonably full lives. So there may be souls in Purgatory, or in Heaven, somehow provided with information and means of action by God. Souls may also come to have different bodies. Very few Christians believe in reincarnation, when a soul takes on a different earthly body. But it is a theoretical possibility, and Christian belief in resurrection seems to suggest taking on a body which is not physically continuous with this earthly one (which decays in the earth).

Christians have never believed that the material body is bad, and that the soul is trapped in it, needing to be liberated by fasting and prayer. That is a typical belief of Gnosticism, from which early Christian thinkers tried to distance themselves. Rather, for Christians the body should be the physical expression of the soul, and each soul is meant to be embodied, in order to learn and to act in a material environment. To be embodied, each soul needs a brain, which has been prepared over millions of years of cosmic evolution precisely for that purpose. Souls then have the responsibility of caring for and guarding their physical environment, and making it a place of beauty and goodness. When that task is done, they pass on to new forms of existence and embodiment, and hopefully to a fuller and more intense knowledge and love of the creator.

## SECOND VIEW: PSYCHO-PHYSICAL UNITY

Many Christians feel that to think of humans as made up of two distinct parts, soul and body, does not take enough account of the unity of the human person. They would stress much more the fully physical nature of human beings, but point out that the physical world may contain many possibilities which are of great spiritual significance. It does not have to be regarded as an accidental play of blind and purposeless forces. On this view, to speak of the human soul is simply to speak of the complex material life-form which is the human being, but to draw attention to its character as a self-conscious, rational and free physical organism.

The soul is not an immaterial substance which is added to the body. Rather, consciousness is a property of a suitably complex and organised physical array, which comes to be able to represent its own environment. Anything with a brain, however primitive, probably has some form of awareness. Cats and dogs are conscious, even though we might not want to say they have immortal souls. Their consciousness is a property of their brains, so that what looks like electrochemical activity in the brain, seen from the outside, actually feels to the brain itself like some sort of conscious perception.

One way of putting this is to say that complex physical individuals like brains have a double aspect. The external aspect is the sort of electrical activity you can observe and record with instruments in a laboratory. The internal aspect is 'what that feels like' to the possessor of the brain. Scientists can now locate which parts of the brain are active when specific perceptions and thoughts occur, so the easiest hypothesis is that the conscious state just *is* the internal aspect of the brain state. So on this view conscious states and brain states are identical. They always go together, and you cannot get one without the other.

Consequently, it might be better not to speak about 'the soul', as though it was a separate thing. We could just say that persons are particularly complex physical organisms which have developed the capacity to think, understand and decide. The soul is, in a sense, what a particular brain/body complex does. But one of the things it can do is to be aware of God, to praise God and to seek to obey God's will. It is in that way that humans come to be images of God, by consciously relating to God and trying to discern the divine purpose in creation.

Christians who take this view will not speak of the soul as immortal, and will not be troubled by the question of when the soul enters or leaves the body, or what it does without a body. Clearly, if it is part of a body/brain complex, it is more sensible to think about the development and decay of what we call personal capacities, like intellectual understanding and moral freedom, a sense of personal continuity, and so on.

Theologians like John Polkinghorne who take a view rather like this prefer to talk of the resurrection of the body than of the immortality of the soul. An image sometimes used is of a computer program which can be taken out of one machine and loaded into another. One might think of the information and memories of a person, and the capacities for programming a body in a specific way, as being abstracted from this earthly body and inserted into another suitably prepared body by God. There would need to be some form of embodiment, and presumably God can provide it. That analogy might be very inadequate, but it helps to convey the general idea that a brain of a specific structure and way of operating could be replicated sufficiently well by God, even if in a different specific form, to be called a 'resurrection' or re-creation of 'the same' brain or person.

It is worth noting that though this 'materialist' view of the human soul may seem very different from the dualist view, the difference does not have many religious consequences. The reason Christians talk about a soul is to affirm that humans are more than assemblages of material particles, and have a special dignity, being worthy of special respect. They are capable of relating to God in a unique way, and their lives possess a value which cannot be taken away. Both views can affirm that, since both see humans as having distinctive capacities – especially that of moral understanding and freedom – which make them worthy of special respect. The Christian answer to the question, 'Why should human life be given a special respect?' is because human consciousness and freedom is given by God, so that each person may responsibly decide on issues which will affect their eternal destiny. Of course, all life is given by God, and so should be respected in very many ways. Human life remains special, however, because humans are intended by God to form a self-conscious, reflective and creative moral community in which each person finds fulfilment by valuing and caring for others. It is this divine intention of reciprocal membership of a self-conscious moral community which requires that each person respects (and loves) other persons as they respect and love themselves.

## THIRD VIEW: THE SOUL AS THE FORM OF THE BODY

There is another view of the nature of the soul which stands somewhere between a dualist and a monist view. It has a good claim to be called the 'classical' view, at least in Western Europe, since it was formulated by Thomas Aquinas in the thirteenth century and has been widely accepted by theologians since. Thomas follows the thought of Aristotle, and Thomas's view might equally well be called qualified materialism or qualified dualism. Aristotle defined the soul, in general, as the principle of life. Vegetables and animals, he thought, had souls – that is, principles of life, which enable them to grow, reproduce and perceive. Humans, however, have 'intellectual souls', which enable them to think abstractly, to have the power of understanding and of acting responsibly. When Aristotle called the soul 'the form of the human body', he was trying to say what the 'form', the essential nature, of humans was, which distinguished them from other animals. This essential nature he found in the power of rational thought. So he was saying that the human body is a body with the distinguishing capacity to think rationally. Humans are essentially rational animals.

It is unclear whether Aristotle thought the capacity for reason was just the capacity of a certain complex material thing, or whether he had some non-material faculty of rational thought in mind. With Aquinas, however, it is clear that the soul becomes a 'substantial form'. That is, rational thought is the essential defining characteristic of human beings, but it requires a non-material faculty which does the rational thinking. For Aquinas, the material brain of itself cannot think. So there must be an immaterial principle which thinks, an active thinking subject. Nevertheless, this subject is not a separate substance (as in unqualified dualism). It is a faculty, even though an immaterial one, of the embodied human being. So Aquinas says, 'I am not my soul'. I am the integrated human person, which has a soul (an immaterial faculty of thought) as my essential defining characteristic.

So for Aquinas each soul is the soul of a particular physical body, and it cannot properly and naturally exist without that body. By a sort of miracle, God can give souls existence without their bodies after death, but only in an improper and unnatural way. The proper destiny of each soul is to be re-united with its own unique body, and so to form a complete person. For Aquinas, then, the human person is essentially a material thing, though it has an important spiritual component or capacity, and that is what makes humans distinctive.

All these Christian views of the human soul differ from some religious views that souls exist without beginning or end, and enter into bodies in a temporary way, or that all souls are parts of one Supreme Soul, into which they should merge. The heart of the Christian view is that each person is quite unique and distinctive, and will remain an individual for as long as God wills. The important thing about humans is that they are free rational agents, capable of sharing in the creative activity of God, so their existence in the universe is not accidental or unplanned. Humans, and any other rational free agents like them, are the reason why this whole cosmos exists. To call them 'souls' is to stress their kinship with the divine, and affirm that they each have a unique role to play in the working out of the divine purpose for creation.

# 5 SIN AND 'THE FALL'

It seems obvious that the divine plan to form a real moral community on earth has been to some extent at least thwarted. There has been a fall from the original divine plan for this planet, and there needs to be a restoration of that plan. The Christian faith is largely concerned with the nature of that 'fall' – which is said to be due to sin – and the nature of the restoration – which is called salvation or redemption. If the first major belief of Christian faith is that God created the universe for a loving purpose, the second is that humans have corrupted that purpose, so that human existence is now lived in estrangement from the being of the Creator. In traditional terms, human beings exist and are born 'in sin'. It is this fact, Christians would say, that shows the need for a Redeemer.

The idea of 'sin' has, for many people, become difficult to understand. In a world in which people are encouraged to do things their own way, and make their own decisions, it has become hard to think of people as under the orders of some all-powerful God, who commands them to do what he wants, and punishes them if they disobey. The atheistic French philosopher Jean-Paul Sartre thought that if humans were going to live truly authentic lives, to be fully human and thus fully free, they must reject any idea of a God who was always watching and judging them. The very idea of God was, he thought, incompatible with human freedom and maturity.

At the same time, and very ironically, Sartre gave what is probably one of the most effective depictions of Hell in modern literature, in his play *Huis Clos*, translated as 'No Exit'. In that play, three characters are shut in a room with each other, and locked in a perpetual battle of hatred and fear. As they look at each other, they see the others either as seeking to devour them, or as objects to be devoured, and so they are torn between fear and contempt. They seek to live their lives through the eyes of the others, to obtain status and regard. But they are condemned to be despised or hated, and can never obtain what they really want, or even fully admit it to themselves. In fact, the doors of the room are not locked, but they are psychologically unable to escape from their destructive relationships, and, in one of the play's best-known lines, Sartre writes that 'Hell is other people'.

In Sartre's play there is no imperious God and no infantile rebellion. But there is a perpetual and inescapable failure to escape from the cycle of hatred and fear which characterises human lives. And that, strangely enough, is very like the New Testament idea of 'sin'. The Greek word for 'sin' (*hamartia*) means 'failing to hit the target'. Human beings are 'in sin', because they fail to hit the target of living as they should. They fail to live authentic, or truly human lives. They destroy one another, and themselves, psychologically and sometimes physically, because they are trapped by their own inadequacies and failures.

There is no God in Sartre's play. But the very fact that if there were a God it would be seen as a commanding, fearful God is itself a reflection of human sin. The whole message of the play is that, when we look at others, what we see is a perverted projection of our own fears and desires. When we see another person as about to devour us, it is our own fear that causes us to see that. When we see another as a victim to be abused, it is our own insecurity and egoism that corrupts our vision. So, when we see God as a tyrannical, vindictive God, it is our own passions that we are projecting onto God.

When Sartre rejects God, it is that perverted vision of God that he rejects. But how then can humans escape from inauthenticity into true human freedom? At that point, Sartre has little to offer, even though he wrote many plays and novels on the subject. It all comes down to the rather banal recommendation, 'Be yourself'. Refuse to live according to convention. Embrace the absurdity of life with pointless passion. Life has no meaning, but each person must invent a meaning for themselves, and live it out in the face of the absurd.

The Christian faith offers a very different vision of human life. We are not created by a vindictive God who is always ordering us about. We are created by a God who has designed the universe so that we can grow to maturity in freedom, be responsible for one another, and learn to understand and appreciate the wisdom and beauty of the universe. God gives us freedom, but always seeks to guide us to a way of life in which that freedom will be used for good. God's 'orders' are not arbitrary commands. They are directions for finding our fulfilment, as personal and moral agents, in understanding, sharing and appreciating the experiences and projects of others.

Authentic life, for the Christian, consists in relating to others in love – rejoicing in their joys, sympathising with their sorrow, co-operating with them in their plans, and helping them in their troubles. We grow most fully when we grow with others in a community of fellowship. For a Christian, authentic life is not 'doing your own thing'. It is living together in creative and compassionate communities. God calls us to live together in love, and helps to make such love possible. Such a God is not a vindictive tyrant, but one who is called 'Father', a compassionate creator who leaves us free but wants us to build up moral and responsible communities.

It is that freedom, however, which has been misused. Sin is a turning away from the call of love towards egoistic desire. We fall into hating and fearing others, because we are not prepared to value them for what they are, and seek their good as much as we seek our own. We become trapped in our search for personal pleasure, so that we cease to think of others as persons at all, and come to see them just as means to our own gratification. That is the 'fall into sin' which

Christians see as marking the whole of human existence. The desire for personal gratification causes us to stop seeing others as persons, and just regard them as things. It is not surprising that, having ceased to love others, we then become unable to accept love from others, and we find ourselves trapped in a world without love and, ultimately, without meaning or value.

Christians accept the Biblical view that humans are made in the image of God, to reflect something, however little, of the creative power, the sensitive knowledge and wisdom, and the universal goodness of God. In the long evolutionary ascent of life, there must have been a first animal, whether it was a member of the species *homo sapiens* or not – which was conscious of its surroundings, which could see that some acts are good and some are bad, which knew for the first time that it ought to do the good, and which had the power to do either the good or the bad. In other words, there must have been a first responsible moral agent in the history of the planet earth.

Most life-forms are not morally responsible. They cannot form the concepts of 'good' and 'bad'. They have no general conception that they 'ought' to do one and avoid the other, and no freedom to choose anyway. Perhaps some of the higher mammals have some sort of moral consciousness. Some people say their dogs know what they should do, and look guilty if they do not do it. But such canine behaviour is hard to distinguish from conditioned training and fear of punishment. If we really think dogs know the difference between right and wrong, and can freely choose which to do, we will regard them as moral agents. But most people might think that, like very young human children, dogs are not fully morally responsible, and need to be trained rather than reasoned with.

There might be quite a wide and fuzzy boundary between conditioned behaviour and a fully responsible moral choice. Nevertheless, there can be no doubt that at one point in time no being on earth had made a moral choice, and at some later time such choices were being made. Agents were fully aware of what they ought to do, and were freely choosing whether or not to do it. This was not just a matter of conditioning and fear of punishment, but a decision about whether or not to perform an act just because one ought to do so.

Christians connect this sense of moral responsibility with the possibility of evolving from the pre-moral behaviour of most animals towards a community of freely self-directing, loving and co-operating moral agents. Human persons are meant to become channels of divine creativity, wisdom, compassion and loving-kindness. But that means that people must freely centre themselves on God and God's will, not on themselves and their own desires. If people are to be free agents, it must be possible for them to refuse to centre their lives on God, and instead seek personal pleasure, status or power, without putting either God or other people first. That is what 'sin' is – putting oneself first.

The 'wages of sin', the Bible says, 'is death' (Romans 6:23). Putting yourself first leads to the breakdown of loving human relationships. It leads to envy, pride, hatred and oppression of others. It makes you unable either to give love to others, or to accept love from them. So in the end you become isolated, alone and without love. Since selfish pleasures always turn out to be ultimately unsatisfying, you become bored and restless. Heroin addicts always need another 'fix', but are never finally satisfied, and are apt to end their days in misery and despair, destroying both their own and other people's lives. That is the way of spiritual death. 'Hell' is the ultimate state of people who have consistently chosen egoism, and who can neither live with other people nor live without them. It is a place wherein people continually torment themselves and each other, a world without love, point or purpose, a world of selfish selves tortured by being forced to live together.

Actual sins are the selfish choices we continually seem to make. But Christians talk about 'original sin', as the state into which we are born, which makes sin, and therefore spiritual death, almost inevitable. Traditionally, there are two components to original sin. There is the fact that we lack clear knowledge of the presence of God. And there is the fact that, largely because of that, we lack the power to do what is right naturally and readily. We have a fatal weakness of will.

Over thousands of generations, so many human beings have made selfish choices that human society has been corrupted. We are all now born into a society where greed and egoism is encouraged by the structures of society, and where the sense of God has been so repressed that it has almost been lost altogether. We are not born on an equal playing-field, with an equal chance of choosing good or bad. We are virtually bound to choose bad, because so many things in society teach us to do so from the moment we are born, and because we lack that close relationship to God which would give us the strength to resist the temptations of egoism. That is the essence of original sin. The human race has cut itself off, by millions of selfish actions by our ancestors, from the power, wisdom and goodness of God.

## FIRST VIEW: ORIGINAL SIN AS INHERITED

Augustine formulated the view which has been common in the West that Adam and Eve, the first humans, were created in innocence, in the Garden of Eden (which means 'the garden of bliss'). They were tempted by Satan, chief of the fallen angels, who had already sinned against God, to claim knowledge before they had learned wisdom (to take the fruit of the tree of knowledge, against the command of God). When they did so, their disobedience was punished by hardship and death (Genesis 3). Their guilt was inherited by their descendants (possibly through sexual intercourse), so all humans are now born in a state of guilt, for which death is the penalty. All humans are thus born in a hopeless condition, unable to obey or love God. They somehow share in the refusal of the first humans to love God, and the whole human race is in rebellion against its creator.

Modern views of this sort do not insist on a literal 'fall' from innocence of Adam and Eve, but still hold that the whole human species is alienated from God, so that every human will is set against its creator and trapped in a web of selfish desire. There is no escape from this situation unless God can somehow set aside this 'original guilt' and change the basic nature of the human will. Augustine's view conflicts with an evolutionary account of human origins, which assumes that suffering and death existed long before the first humans existed. The Darwinian account also denies that acquired characteristics can be inherited, so that later generations could not inherit a guilt that Adam himself had acquired. There is in addition a severe moral difficulty about holding that every human being is born guilty, before they have actually done anything.

More modern versions of a generally Augustinian view, however, might hold that humans might have been exempt from death (perhaps naturally passing to an immortal state from earthly life) if they had not sinned. Certainly, they might not have seen bodily death as a great and fearful evil, and might have had a natural knowledge that their lives would continue with God. Further, it might be said that the doctrine of original guilt simply states the truth that all humans are born with fatally weakened wills, which would lead them to destruction if it were not for the forgiving grace of God.

## SECOND VIEW: ORIGINAL SIN AS ESTRANGEMENT

A modified view is that held, for instance, by the twentieth-century philosopher F.R. Tennant. Consistent with evolutionary theory, it holds that the first humans (or the first morally responsible agents, whoever they were) were indeed innocent, not yet having made a moral choice. They were, however, subject to hardship, conflict and death, like other mammals. They might well have been lustful and aggressive, like most successful evolved species. When the first moment of responsible moral choice came, it was perhaps only a sense that one should not kill so many enemies, or not torture all captives quite so much. What was in question was a slow, gradual moralisation of primal human desires. The first humans could have consistently chosen what they perceived to be good, however morally flawed it may seem to us. If they had done so, human history would have been very different. Perhaps the sense of God's presence would have grown in a strong and continuous way, and God would have helped them always to make good and creative choices.

But they in fact chose egoism. This choice spread through the societies of their descendants, until the whole human race was locked into a course of egoistic choices. The sense of God's presence faded, and humans cut themselves off from grace, from the divine power to do the good without difficulty. 'Original sin' is the state of estrangement from God and weakness of will which is caused by the failure of early hominids to grow morally as they should have done. Now it is almost impossible to realise the proper goal of human life, since each human life is part of a society ruled by greed, hatred and desire.

## THIRD VIEW: ORIGINAL SIN AS A NECESSARY STAGE IN EVOLUTION

A more radical interpretation, taken by theologians like Paul Tillich, is that estrangement from God is necessary to human existence in freedom. It might be said that humans cannot be truly free unless they are free from an intense, even overpowering, sense of the omnipotent God. Moreover, lust and aggression are necessary if humans are to survive in the face of competition from other species in the evolutionary struggle. So egoism and conflict are inevitable, as part of an evolutionary growth towards the society of justice and peace which God ultimately wills. Individuals are not born either depraved (the first view) or doomed to failure (the second view). No one is guilty unless they actually do something wrong, and no one is forced to do wrong. But, because of their evolutionary past, humans do exist in societies in which egoism and conflict are inevitable, so that a society of perfect compassion and co-operation is impossible. There is a necessary moral imperfection and a lack of God-consciousness in human society. This could be called 'original sin'. It is not due to something that happened in the past, but it is the present condition of being alienated from God. It is certainly a condition from which one needs to be delivered, if there is to be any possibility of a compassionate, just and equitable society in which humans can fully express their creative and co-operative dispositions.

For all these different interpretations of original sin, the human situation is desperate. Humans have a sense of what they ought to do, and of how they ought to live. But they can never do as they ought. They seem to be trapped in their own selfish desires, and they lack a strong sense of the presence of God which might give them the strength to escape. God is the only one who can 'save' humanity, who can liberate human life from the greed, hatred and anger which dominates so much of human life, and makes existence seem like a form of Hell.

Christians are quite clear that God is the only Saviour. But do human beings need any saviour? Can they not save themselves? The reason they cannot, Christians would say, is that salvation – wholeness of life – only properly comes when a loving relationship to God is established. And only God can take the initiative in establishing such a relationship. It is God who liberates from egoism, who invites into a relationship of love, and who gives the divine love to humans to enable them to respond adequately to that invitation. Christians would say that an important part of the history of humanity is the story of how God seeks to liberate humans from selfish desire and invites them to share in the power of the divine love.

# 6 JESUS, THE INCARNATION OF GOD

If God is to be the Saviour of 'fallen' humanity, then God must act to show humans the nature of sin, to show them the divine love, and to liberate people from sin. On the planet earth, Christians believe that God acted to do this specifically in the person of Jesus. That is why the person of Jesus is central to Christian faith. It matters to Christians that God should really have acted in Jesus, that Jesus should have said and done the things which are attributed to him in the Gospels, and that we have a reliable record of the acts of God in Jesus. This has raised problems for some people, who do not see how human salvation can be made to depend on knowledge of historical facts which happened a long time ago, and may well be disputed by historians. Can we really have enough knowledge of the history of Jesus to be sure that it happened as it is recorded? And can our salvation really depend on having such knowledge?

The question about our historical knowledge of Jesus is not one that is unique to Christianity. Virtually every religious tradition has a founding teacher or prophet, who is regarded with special reverence as the originator of a particular way of spiritual understanding. Usually, the lives of the founders are depicted in a heroic and highly symbolic fashion. Their mighty deeds are portrayed as virtually superhuman exploits, and filled with cosmic significance. So for example, Gautama Buddha is said to have been miraculously born and to have performed many miraculous acts. Krishna is said to have balanced a mountain in his hands. And Jesus, the originator of the Christian way, is said to have been miraculously born of a virgin, to have walked on water, turned water into wine, and raised Lazarus from the dead. Most astonishing of all, he appeared to and talked with his disciples after he had been killed.

The problem for the historian is to assess the accuracy of such accounts. In the Christian case, there is at least one virtually certain fact – that soon after the death of Jesus, a number of people, led by an inner group, 'the Twelve', believed that he was the designated Messiah of Israel, the one chosen by God to be king in a new Messianic age of peace and justice. There is not much reason to disbelieve the main features of his story, as presented in the four Gospels in the New Testament. He was a wandering teacher from the northern province of Galilee, who only visited the capital city, Jerusalem, once or twice. He gained a reputation for exorcising demons, healing the sick, and getting into arguments with the religious authorities. He ruthlessly criticised the pride and legalism of some of the Pharisees (with whose beliefs he in general identified). He seemed to possess an intense personal experience of the reality and Fatherhood of God. He astonished people by his authoritative exposition of the Scriptures and his wisdom in piercing to the secrets of the heart. He ate and drank with tax collectors, prostitutes and other social outcasts. He taught forgiveness, compassion, humility and loving-kindness to all without distinction of race or gender, a non-judgemental attitude to others, and a vivid hope for the rule of God in human life. He attracted a group of disciples, and appointed twelve of them to call the people of Israel to repentance, and to proclaim that the 'kingdom of God' was at hand. After only about three years, however, he was put to death as a political or religious trouble-maker. By far the longest sections of the Gospels are devoted to an account of his 'passion', the story of the insults and cruelty he endured as he was betrayed, brought before the authorities, and condemned to death. In these crucial days, his followers deserted him. He died and was buried.

That might have been the end of the story. But after that, a number of his disciples had a series of visions or experiences which led them to believe that he had been raised from death by God, and designated the Messianic king. And that was the beginning of the Christian Church.

There have been many fanciful attempts to reconstruct the actual historical Jesus, but it is impossible to discount the fact that the only records we have are the Gospels, written by people who believed he was the Messiah (the Christ, in Greek). These are not neutral records. They are collections of oral traditions, stories and teachings, which are meant to present Jesus as the Christ. The historian would therefore expect them to be strongly biased. But that does not mean they are inaccurate – one can have an account of the life of Churchill which is very biased in his favour, but which presents all the facts accurately. What some would call 'bias' would be seen by others as the most adequate interpretation. In fact I think one can say that no history is totally neutral. All interesting history includes interpretation. So it is important to be clear about one's presuppositions.

Take first the case of someone who thinks there is no God, and who thinks all the prophets of Israel were deluded. When they read the Gospels, they will naturally think that their writers were deluded, so the whole history will be infected by error, root and branch. In particular, the miracles – the exorcisms, healings and power over natural elements, the virgin birth and the resurrection – are legends. Jesus was most probably a mistaken prophet of a Jewish revival which never came, and his life ended in failure. The church begins with a number of illusory experiences that his disorientated followers had. There is not much point trying to get back to the real historical Jesus, because the only accounts we have of his life have been completely overlaid with legends and illusions.

Now take the opposite extreme, and think of someone who, in their own personal experience, has encountered a life-giving spiritual presence which has come to them as they accepted the teaching that Jesus, in a glorified spiritual form of existence, is alive and active in the lives of men and women today. When they read the Gospels, they will be prepared to accept that the accounts of the appearances of the risen Jesus are genuine. Belief in Jesus as the Christ is not a delusion. Because they think that God genuinely seeks to manifest the truth of his love in Jesus, they will expect that the accounts of the life of Jesus, which show this truth, are accurate in all important respects. If miracles are recorded there, they will be ready to accept their occurrence, because after all Jesus is the revelation of God in history, and they will expect such a revelation to make an extraordinary difference to normal human events. If Jesus rose uniquely from the dead, it would not be so surprising if his birth was also unique. So it is quite understandable that one can have completely different interpretations of the same Gospels, just because of the different presuppositions which readers take to the text.

## FIRST VIEW: A SYMBOLIC CHRISTOLOGY

Christians are people who take Jesus as the originator of their spiritual way, so they are obviously not going to regard the Gospels as products of delusion. Even among Christians, however, there are very different ways of interpreting the person of Jesus, as it is presented in the Gospels. The minimalist account seeks to work with as little historical material as possible. It is not denied that Jesus existed, gained a reputation among his followers as a healer and religious teacher of great power and authority, and died by crucifixion. It may well be said that he must have been the sort of person whom it was reasonable for the disciples to accept as the expected Christ – a good man of intense religious conviction and utter devotion to God. Nevertheless, a good many, perhaps nearly all, of the Gospel records are legendary or symbolic rather than factual.

A number of reasons can be given for this. First, there are no demons to be exorcised, so all accounts of exorcisms are based on false factual beliefs about the causes of illness. Second, the general laws of nature are not interrupted by miracles, so the accounts of

Jesus' miracles are the result of attempts to magnify his powers – and he may indeed have been a faith-healer – to supernatural dimensions. Third, the great differences between the Gospels, particularly between the first three Synoptic Gospels and the Fourth Gospel of John, are such that they cannot all give an accurate representation of the historical Jesus. In the Synoptic Gospels, for instance, Jesus speaks in parables, does not openly declare himself as Messiah, and refers to himself as 'Son of Man'. In John's Gospel, however, he speaks in long discourses, openly declaring himself to be the Son of God, and claims a unique relationship with God the Father. There are also differences in the order of events recorded, and in many details like the day of the Last Supper or the genealogy of Jesus.

So it might be said that each Gospel presents a rather different imaginative theological reflection on the life of Jesus, as it was seen in the light of the visionary experiences of the risen Christ in the early churches. For this interpretation, the Christian faith really began with a set of vivid experiences and visions by the apostles after the death of Jesus. In these visions, they believed that they encountered Jesus himself, raised from death by God, and felt the power of the Holy Spirit which he gave to them, filling them with new hope and joy. The risen and glorified Christ who was encountered in the experience of the early church is then projected back onto the historical Jesus, giving that life a more magical and momentous feel than it probably had in fact.

For such a view, what Christians now have to work with is not so much the historical Jesus as four rather different portraits of the Christ which took shape in the early church. These portraits are portraits of a historical person. They are not simply made up out of visions or dreams. Just as an icon is based on a real person, but is stylised in a particular way, so the Gospel portraits are based on the historical Jesus, but are stylised to form icons, ways of expressing the image of the nature of God, and the character of the action of God, which have been discerned in Jesus after years of prayerful reflection.

When Christians relate to Jesus today, they often do so through some picture of a bearded, long-haired man, or through a picture of

a bleeding body on a cross, or through the symbol of a figure opening its breast to display its heart. It is not at all certain – some would
say, it is obviously false – that these pictures are anything like the historical Jesus at all. But that does not matter. Icons have their own
spiritual power, and while they do relate to the historical figure of
Jesus, all that we need to know is that God did indeed manifest the
divine nature through that figure. The ways in which we now represent it to ourselves are primarily for our benefit, and in terms that
appeal to us.

The historical Jesus lived and died. Out of his life, and the impres-
sion it made on his followers, an icon, or a number of icons, of the
divine nature in human form were constructed within the early
church communities. His life was seen as a perfect exemplification of
Torah, of the life fully obedient to God, and as a manifestation of the
forgiving love of God itself. His death was seen as an expression of a
divine love which would go to any lengths to reconcile human lives
to God. The triumphant king of Messianic expectation became the
suffering king who gives his life for his people. The experiences of
the Spirit which came to the disciples after his death were seen as a
manifestation of the redeeming and reconciling act of God. Here a
new covenant was made between God and human beings, now
extended to the whole human race. And a new way of liberation from
evil, by accepting the life-giving power of the Holy Spirit, was established. Thus, even though the life of Jesus has passed beyond historical recall, out of that life has grown an image of the suffering and
redeeming love of God, which can become a channel of that love to
human beings in many times and places. The life of Jesus evoked in
the community of disciples a set of closely related icons of the love of
God which have the power to make God known and to make God's
love effective for millions of people who never knew the historical
Jesus.

Those who hold such a view of Jesus, like the British theologian
John Hick, would probably regard the classical doctrine of the
Incarnation as a 'myth' or 'metaphor'. To speak of a literal incarnation

would be to say that God, or the Son of God, actually took form as a human being and walked the earth as a man. One could regard that doctrine as a myth, while still holding that the human person of Jesus expresses a perfect human relationship to God, or even perfectly expresses in a human life what God's own love is like. Moreover, God might act through the life of Jesus in a special way to inaugurate a new way of liberation from evil. So Jesus would retain a central importance for human salvation, and could be a unique way of showing what God is and effecting God's action in the world. Yet he would not literally be God walking and talking in Galilee.

For that reason, it is not so important to have an exact historical record of his words and actions, as though they were the very words and actions of God, and essential for human salvation. What is important is to have an insight into God's nature as love, and to have a personal experience of God's liberating power. The portrayal of Jesus in the Gospels is capable of giving that insight and conveying that experience, even if it is not an exact record of historical facts. It is the portrait which matters, and the experience it evokes and sustains, not the literal historical accuracy of the New Testament accounts. Such Christians can legitimately say that they believe in the doctrine of the Incarnation, though not in a literal sense.

## SECOND VIEW: A DIVINE MAN CHRISTOLOGY

Many Christians would find such a minimalist and metaphorical view far from satisfactory. They would want to place much more reliability on the Gospel accounts. There is, they might say, a Devil and there are demons. Miracles do occur, and by means of them God shows that Jesus is master of the forces of darkness and of the natural world. Indeed, they would think it quite inadequate to start by thinking of Jesus as some sort of local preacher or faith-healer. One must begin, they would say, by seeing that God had been preparing Israel over many generations for a unique and unprecedented occurrence, for the Incarnation of God himself in human form. It is entirely appropriate that such a unique incarnation should be manifested in a supernatural birth, miraculously caused by the Holy Spirit, without a human father. When the prophets looked for a Messianic deliverer they were, even if they did not fully realise it, preparing the way for the coming of the eternal Son of God into human history.

It is true that God revealed something of the divine nature in many different cultures. But all the time God was preparing the ground for one decisive revelation in a human person. God did not just speak words through a prophet, or make himself known in inner experience, or in mighty acts of liberation in history. God actually 'became flesh', taking form as a human being, so that he would fully share in the human condition, and be known by human beings in the fullest possible way. Of course God is not a human being. Nor does God turn into a human being, as though he ceased to be the ruler and sustainer of the universe. God exists without beginning or end, as the creator of the universe, omnipotent and omniscient. But that God, without changing in his essential nature, can take to himself a human nature, so that he also acts and experiences as a man.

It is rather as if a human being could, without losing any of his human powers, appear, act and experience as an animal – say, a bear – in a community of bears. That would mean restraining most of his human powers, but he would when necessary be able to use his human knowledge and wisdom to enable that bear to do things that would be well beyond the power or understanding of other bears. In an analogous way, God could choose to be born and act and die as a man, restraining his divine powers for most of the time. Yet because he is omnipotent and omniscient, he could miraculously heal the sick, command the elements to obey him, and rise from the dead by his own divine power.

On this account, defended in recent years by Richard Swinburne and Thomas Morris, Jesus is God in human form. He has both a divine mind, which is omniscient and omnipotent, and a human mind, which is finite in knowledge and power. The human mind does not have full access to the divine mind, though it is natural to think that it will have an access greater than that of any other human being. The divine mind, however, has full access to the human mind, and ensures that the human mind always thinks and acts in accordance with the divine will. Thus the ultimate causal agent in the life of Jesus is the divine mind, even though the human mind makes its own decisions within the limits placed on it by the divine mind. Both minds, it must be stressed, are united in a unique way, in the one 'person' of Jesus Christ, so that Jesus is, in the words of the Council of Chalcedon (451CE) true God and true man, two natures in one person.

The early church made this point by insisting on calling his mother Mary, who was already believed to have been a virgin when she conceived, not only the mother of the man Jesus, but 'the mother of God' – meaning, of course, the mother of God in his human form, not God in his eternal nature. Why would God take on, or assume, human nature? Partly, perhaps, because in this way God could give the fullest possible revelation of himself to humans. Not only would the life of Jesus show what God was like; it would actually *be* the life of God itself (again, the church made this point by saying that Jesus was not just like God, but was 'of one substance with' God). This would be the fullest possible sharing by God in the human condition.

An even stronger reason for the Incarnation is that God would be uniting human nature to the divine nature in the closest possible way. When Jesus died and rose from death, he was liberating human nature from death and separation from God. In him the estrangement of humanity from God was decisively and completely overcome. He becomes the Saviour of humanity, the one who saves us from estrangement and eternal separation from God, because in himself he unites humanity to God for ever, and he has the power to unite our humanity to God as well.

For such Christians, the heart of the Christian faith is that God the creator has actually united human nature to the divine nature, has entered into human history at a particular point in the person of Jesus of Nazareth, and has thereby promised that humanity itself will be assumed into the closest possible relation to divinity. When God enters into history, he extends the covenant with Abraham and his descendants to all humanity, inviting all people into a fully personal relationship with Jesus Christ. He fulfilled and transcended Torah in the perfect human life of Jesus, which from henceforth becomes the pattern of human living. He decisively delivers humanity from separation from God. And he founds the Messianic kingdom, not as a renewed nation of Israel, but as the inner rule of Jesus Christ in the hearts of all who turn to him in faith.

## THIRD VIEW: A SPIRIT CHRISTOLOGY

The belief that Jesus is a totally unique God-man, that he is the omnipotent and omniscient God restraining or perhaps temporarily giving up his powers while he takes the form of a man, is a very traditional form of Christian belief. It seems quite a long way from the belief that Jesus was a prophet and teacher who evoked an icon of the divine nature in the experience of the early church. But there is an intermediate position, found for instance in the twentieth-century Scottish theologian Donald Baillie, which tries to incorporate insights from both these beliefs. It emphasises the traditional point (made at the Council of Chalcedon) that Jesus is fully and truly human. Thus he is genetically a human being, who learns a language and beliefs from his culture, like any other human being, and whose powers and abilities are those properly belonging to human beings. He is not omniscient – for no truly human being could have knowledge of what happens on the other side of the universe, for example – and he is not omnipotent – for no human being can fly or literally move mountains.

What is distinctive about Jesus is that he is a human being whose life is filled with the Spirit of God in a uniquely intense and intimate way. The prophets were filled with the Spirit when they prophesied. But such inspiration lasted only a short time, and applied only to the words they spoke, or sometimes to special actions they felt impelled to perform. Jesus' whole life was filled with the Spirit from beginning to end, and the Spirit affected absolutely everything he said and did.

This means that Jesus was a man who lived in a close and intense awareness of the presence of God, and who freely allowed his life to be directed by the Spirit.

In one sense, any human being can become a vehicle of the Spirit of God, and a perfect human life would consist in being such a vehicle at all times. Such a life would be 'without sin', for it would never be estranged from God, and would never act against the will of God. The wisdom of such a person would certainly be greater than that of almost everyone else he met, and perhaps the Spirit would be able to act through him to heal many forms of mental and bodily illness, since he would be a medium of the acts of God. If miracles are occurrences which transcend the normal physical regularities of the physical order, and which convey spiritual power, then such a life might well be attended by the occurrence of miracles.

From one point of view, Jesus is an especially intense case of a perfected, Spirit-filled human life, though not necessarily an absolutely unique one. But there is more to Jesus than that. He is empowered by the Spirit of God to be a morally and spiritually perfect human being. But he is also designated, by the will of God, as the Messianic king whom the prophets had foretold. That means he is the man who is to take the Abrahamic covenant and extend it to all humanity, who is to replace the external Law by the internal rule of the Spirit, who is to open up a new path of union with God, and who is to be head of the new community, the church, which is meant to bring peace and justice to the earth.

But is this not still a man, however closely related to God, even though he rules in the place of God in the Messianic kingdom? Jesus is more than a divinely designated human Messiah. He is certainly a man, but his relationship to God is such that he is the very image of God's nature on earth, and his earthly life is the temporal expression of the character of God. In and through him, God acts to liberate humans from their estrangement and despair into a life of companionship and hope. Thus he is the image and act of God, in a way which is uniquely shaped by God, because of its special place in human history. Therefore one can speak of Jesus as having a unique form of unity with God, which, because he possessed it by divine grace, from the beginning and indissolubly, can be called a 'unity of being'. One can say that Jesus is God made manifest in human form.

On this view, Jesus was not the omnipotent omniscient God walking the earth in human form. He was a perfected, Spirit-filled man, who was designated by God to be the prophesied Messianic king, and the very image and act of God in human form. He will remain for all time the normative human image of God and the vehicle of God's saving acts, and as such he can properly be an object of worship and devotion – for what one truly worships is the infinite God in the form of the image that God has designated.

So, in various ways Christians have tried to spell out what they mean by saying that the founder of their spiritual way, Jesus, is not just a sage, mystic or prophet, but is the 'image' or the 'son' of God. The expression 'Son of God' should not, on any of these views, be taken in a physical sense, as though God had a physical son. It must be remembered that Jesus is also spoken of in the Bible as the 'word' and 'wisdom' of God. These are all metaphors which seek to express the unique sort of unity there was between Jesus and the creator. To say that Jesus is the son of God is to say that he is a man chosen by God to be in a unique historical relationship with God, and through whom God can convey that relationship to others. Jesus has a unique role in the history of the earth. That role is to open up a new way of relationship to God, a way which, Christians believe, opens up the way of the Hebrew prophets to the whole world. Christians believe that Jesus is not just a teacher or a revealer of God. He is in some sense the son of God and the Saviour of the world, and that is what makes him unique in human history.

# 7 ATONEMENT

I t is very natural for people to think that there is a creator of the universe – the belief exists in virtually every known human society. If there is such a creator, a mind of great wisdom and power, which has a purpose in creating the universe, it is natural to think that the creator will do something to make that purpose known, or to communicate what it is to created agents. In other words, one might expect that the creator will reveal something of its nature and purpose to finite conscious beings who are part of that purpose. If, as Christians think, the purpose has been frustrated in some way, and needs to be restored, there is even more reason to expect a divine revelation which can make clear what has gone wrong, which can begin to liberate humans from selfish desire and enable them to share in the divine love.

Such a liberation and participation in the divine love is what Christians describe as 'salvation'. To hope for 'salvation' is to hope for some action by God, the creator of human nature, to liberate humans from desire, ignorance and pride, imbue them with compassion, wisdom and humility, and embrace them within a conscious loving relationship with one another and with God. The Christian 'gospel', the good news, is that God has acted, and continues to act, in and through the person of Jesus, to liberate human lives from the power of sin and unite them to God. That is what is meant by saying that Jesus is the Saviour of the world.

Christians all agree on that fact, but the New Testament contains many different metaphors and images to try to explain how God is acting in Jesus, and how God saves humanity through him. As many generations of Christians have reflected on those images, three main accounts of 'the atonement' – that is, the 'at-one-ing' or 'making one' of God and humanity – have taken shape.

## FIRST VIEW: ATONEMENT AS VICTORY

One of the earliest accounts is found in some early Greek-speaking theologians like the fourth-century Gregory of Nyssa. It begins with the thought that humans are slaves of the Devil, who is 'the Lord of this world'. When the first humans disobeyed God, they were following Satan, an angel created by God who disobeyed God, and then tempted the first humans to disobey God also. When Adam and Eve did so, they fell under the control of Satan, who takes them on a path which can only lead to destruction.

Christ is the Son of God, the eternal Wisdom of God who is omnipotent and indestructible. But he comes to earth as a man, as Jesus of Nazareth. He takes the form of a weak and limited human being, and Satan is deceived into thinking that he has Jesus in his power. Jesus offers his life as a 'ransom' in return for the lives of human beings. The Devil is tricked into thinking that he can over-power Jesus. He accepts the bargain, and thinks he has triumphed when he causes Jesus to be crucified. However, as Son of God, Jesus cannot be defeated by death. He rises from death and achieves a decisive victory over the Devil, since he has successfully freed human beings from their slavery to Satan. By that decisive act of resurrection, the powers of evil are conquered. Satan continues to rule on earth, but he has forfeited his power, and when all those humans whom God chooses have been saved (and Gregory thought God would save everyone), Satan and all those who choose to follow him will be cast down to Hell, until eventually even they will be redeemed.

To most people today, this account is too obviously mythical to be accepted as it stands. But it is a symbolic story which conveys important spiritual insights. The image of a hero who offers to fight to save the world, who gives his life in apparent defeat, but who triumphs over evil precisely by that act of renunciation, is a powerful one (in modern times it is found in the role of Obi-Wan Kenobi, in *Star Wars*).

A modern interpretation has been provided by the Lutheran theologian Gustaf Aulen, in his book, *Christus Victor*. The battle between the Devil and the Son of God is the battle between the forces of egoism, which are deeply built into the structures of human social life, and so seem much more than merely individual, and the power of loving compassion, which is the character of God. God gives himself in that God enters into and shares all the pain and suffering of human experience. This is not really a ransom paid to some captor, but it is a high price paid by God so that humans can be delivered from the power of egoism. Only self-giving love can triumph over egoism, which is in the end self-destructive. Jesus is the one who manifests in history the compassionate love of God. His death on the Cross manifests the suffering love of God, which endures all in order to liberate human lives from sin. His resurrection from death is the triumph of love, which is stronger than death. In the end, after many apparent failures, the love of God will eliminate evil and unite to God for ever all who respond to God's offer of forgiveness and healing.

The battle between good and evil was won by Jesus, the Son of God. God now offers to all people a promise of a share in that victory, if they will turn from evil, and accept the power of the risen Christ in their lives. Our individual liberation lies in the future, when God's love will reign supreme. But it begins now, as God takes on himself all the suffering we inflict on others, forgives us, comes near to us in the person of Jesus Christ, and begins to transform us into his victorious image. The emphasis on this interpretation is on the resurrection of Christ, seen as the victory of divine love, a love which gives itself in suffering on the cross so that the power of evil may be destroyed at its heart.

## SECOND VIEW: ATONEMENT AS SACRIFICE

In the Middle Ages a rather different interpretation of the atonement arose, largely due to the great theologian Anselm, the eleventh-century Archbishop of Canterbury. Much more emphasis was placed on the death of Jesus, and this was interpreted as a sacrifice which propitiates for the sins of the world. All human beings sin, and so they owe God a satisfaction for sin. Because they have corrupted the divine purpose and thereby brought so much harm to creation, they need to make reparation for their sin. Unfortunately, however, they can never make such reparation, because they simply do not have the means to do so. When God the Word becomes man in Jesus, Jesus can offer reparation to God on behalf of others, because his own life, being the life of God in human form, is both sinless and of literally infinite value. Therefore the merits of his sacrifice can be passed on to others. Jesus, who is both God and man, makes the reparation to God that other humans cannot make, and thereby he is able to procure forgiveness of sins for all who repent and trust in him.

In a slightly different version of this model, associated with the sixteenth-century Reformer John Calvin, all humans ought to be punished for their sins. But since sin is against an infinitely good God, they deserve an infinite punishment – which they can never complete. Jesus, being both divine and human, can pay an infinite price, and so Jesus takes the punishment due to all humans, and they can be declared forgiven by God.

This interpretation, in both its forms, can seem just a little too mechanical and legalistic to many people. But it retains a stress on the seriousness of sin. God cannot just overlook sin, as though it had never happened. It points up the fact that humans can never really pay back all the harm their sin has done to others, to creation, and to God. And it insists that in Jesus God himself has paid the price of sin, so that people can find forgiveness.

There is a deep attraction in the thought that God himself has paid the price of sin, and that on the cross God in some way takes the just judgement on sin himself, thereby freeing us from the impossible task of making ourselves righteous by our own efforts. When we do wrong, there is nothing of our own we can offer to God to put things right. In that situation of helplessness, God freely gives us the means with which to procure forgiveness. That means is the death of his Son. In forms of piety which centre on the crucified Jesus, we see the self-giving of God, which frees us from the terrible guilt we some-times feel, and assures us that God has gone to the uttermost lengths to bring us back to the divine life.

## THIRD VIEW: ATONEMENT AS HEALING

There is another sort of interpretation which focuses not on the Cross nor on the Resurrection, but on the sending of the Holy Spirit at Pentecost. For this view the basic problem is that sin has locked human beings into mutually destructive lives of hatred and greed, from which they cannot escape. Sin is like a disease which brings with it a moral disability, an inherent weakness of will, which makes people unable to respond to the love of God. What is needed is a way to heal that dis-ability, to strengthen human wills with a power beyond their own, and to help them truly turn to God to receive that power. It is the Holy Spirit who can do that, but the Spirit has to be given in a particular way and in a recognisable form. The life of Jesus was a life filled with the Spirit, and in his life the Spirit was expressed in a recognisable and particular form, the form of self-giving, reconciling love.

Jesus himself forgave sins, and this was associated with healing and reconciling humans to God. It is the whole life of Jesus, com-pletely offered to God to be a vehicle of divine will, which is the channel of the healing power of the Spirit. That life of self-giving comes to a climax, and has its central motivating power expressed, in the Cross, when Jesus gave himself even to death, so that the kingdom of God might come. But it is when the Spirit came on the disciples with power that they experienced the deliverance from sin which is true forgiveness.

God does not insist on the exact payment of some penalty for wrong-doing. Rather God attacks the very source of wrong-doing, in the corruption of the heart, and begins the work of healing there. There is not a magical attainment of immediate perfection. But there is a re-orientation of the heart towards God, an inner, continuing, empowerment by a love that is more than human, and a promise that the heart will eventually be fully conformed to that human image of God which is seen in Jesus. Forgiveness is not just remission of some external penalty. It is a release from the bondage of hatred and greed, a release which guarantees freedom, but which will need to be slowly realised in the life of the sinner who has been met by divine grace, where perhaps only divine judgement was expected.

This third view, often associated with the twelfth-century theologian Abelard, has sometimes been caricatured as merely a 'moral example' view, which regards Jesus just as the example of a perfectly good life which we should follow. It is much more than that, however. It is a view which sees the heart of redemption as lying in an actual transformation of life by the power of the Spirit of God. The Spirit that was fully in Jesus is to work also in us, to conform us however slowly to his image. The Spirit's nature is fully and normatively expressed in the Cross, the symbol of the total self-giving of Jesus to the divine will. The Cross, on this view, is not a death which was necessary to take away the divine anger. But it is the culmination and paradigm expression of a life which is the true expression of the divine love. The Cross was necessary because the love of God is met with hostility by the egoism of human creatures, and it meets this hostility with self-renouncing love. Sin condemns and destroys itself. God offers reconciliation, compassion and forgiveness, and that is what the cross expresses.

These three accounts of atonement are different, but they do not contradict one another, unless taken extremely narrowly. They offer differing perspectives on the common belief that in the life, death and resurrection of Jesus, God offers human beings release from the crippling effects of hatred, greed and egoism. At that point of human history, Christians claim, the way of release and liberation is made clear.

# 8 REVELATION AND THE WORLD RELIGIONS

C hristians believe that Jesus is the supreme revealer of the nature and purpose of God, and the Saviour through whom God liberates humans from sin. But is Jesus the only person who reveals God, and how can that revelation be known by people who have never known him, who live at very different places and times?

God is revealed in Jesus as a God of universal love, who desires people to turn from sin and accept the divine love into their lives. Jesus often speaks of God as seeking out sinners, just as a shepherd might look for a lost sheep (Luke 15:3–7), or as a father might welcome the return of a prodigal son (Luke 15:11–24). If God is like that, it seems almost certain that God would somehow make himself known at many times and in many places, in many different ways. It seems unlikely that God should fail to disclose something of his nature and purpose to millions of human beings, who have never heard of Jesus. So it is quite likely that there is some revelation of God at many points in history.

When one looks at human history, one finds that there are indeed many claims to divine revelation – in fact the problem is that there are too many, since they do not all agree on what that revelation is! Many of the wisest and most virtuous human beings have claimed some experience of a spiritual reality, and if one is disposed to think that there is such a reality, one must give such claims a high initial credence. In fact one needs to account for two things – the fact that so many intelligent, sane and virtuous people claim experience of a spiritual reality, and the fact that they often disagree on the precise nature of that reality, and its relation to human beings. We can best account for both these things if we take the view that many saints, sages and prophets do in fact have a genuine experience of God, but that their descriptions of his nature are partial and fallible, being influenced very much by the beliefs and histories of their own cultures.

So, for example, the Christian may accept that the shamans and holy men and women of primal faiths in tribal or pre-literate societies experience what is in fact God. But they interpret that experience in terms of their own general beliefs and value-systems. So they interpret the object of their spiritual experiences as encounter with various quasi-natural spiritual powers which interact in good and bad ways with their tribe. They may not clearly form the idea that there is just one creator – God – though they have the idea that the whole world depends upon some spiritual reality, which interacts with it in important ways. They may not see that God requires justice and mercy, though they may well feel that certain ways of life are required of them, and that they are responsible for their conduct to suprahuman powers.

Naturally enough, Christians will hold that the revelation of God in Jesus is a fulfilment of many other views, which do not see God as a loving Saviour who promises eternal life to all people. But they may also see primal traditions as containing insights which Christians may tend to overlook. For instance, many primal traditions have a sense of the sacredness of nature and of the unity of all life which has a renewed importance for the ecological crisis of our times. There is much to learn from the insights that other cultures and traditions have into the supreme spiritual reality which Christians know as the God and Father of Jesus Christ.

There is much in primal religion which most Christians would find repellent – human sacrifice, bloody initiation rites and permission to enslave whole sections of humanity cannot be regarded as significant insights into the nature of God. But one must remember that there is much in Christian history, too, which seems repugnant: the torture of heretics, the forcible conversion of whole nations and the censorship of great works of literature are not things of which most Christians would be proud today. Religion is always a rather ambiguous phenomenon. So no one will want to say that everything in religion is true and helpful. Perhaps many things are misleading and even harmful. What we must do is make sure that we eliminate the misleading things from our own faith, and learn from other faiths the good things they have to tell. That is, after all, what one would expect from a faith like Christianity which preaches universal love and understanding, and which is committed to believing that God is omnipresent.

One could, like Sir James Frazer in *The Golden Bough*, see all primal religious practices as either magical techniques which simply do not work, or attempts to propitiate imagined spiritual forces, which do not work either. But one might take a much more positive view, and see at least some such practices as means of disclosing a spiritual dimension to experienced reality, and relating members of the tribe in a positive and fulfilling way to it. If God is at work in such cults, God is not communicating infallible information, in the form of specific truths. But the reality of Spirit could be influencing human minds, partly in dreams, visions and inspired utterances, to construct effective symbols which enable individuals to participate in a higher spiritual reality. God takes the material of dreams, images and words, which originate in particular cultures and traditions, and enables them to become vehicles of the divine presence and moral power.

So one might see revelation as a divine influence on the minds and imaginations of holy men and women, leading them to new insights into the reality of Spirit, along paths unique to their own particular cultures. Many different religious paths develop, as small tribal groups expand into nations and empires, and continue the process of reflection upon their inherited factual and moral beliefs. These paths have sometimes hardened into opposed systems of belief and practice, and there have even been wars between opposing sets of religious beliefs. One should not, however, exaggerate the role of religion in such wars, which have taken place between ethnic and national groups throughout history, whether or not religion is involved. Religion is more often a tool of imperialist ambitions than a cause of conflict. Nevertheless, it is a fact that religions have often confronted one another as enemies, and vied for supremacy.

In the modern world the situation has changed, because of the vast increase in communications, the ease of travel, and the growth of economic networks of interdependence around the globe. Religions can no longer afford to confront one another as totalising cultural frameworks ('Christendom' versus 'the Islamic world', for example). Every major religion has adherents throughout the world, and different traditions live alongside one another, so that they have to learn more positive ways of working together.

At the heart of most religions is the command to seek peace, justice and fraternity, so this growing together is not something alien to faith at all. But it does require a real respect for and willingness to learn from religious traditions other than one's own. There is no reason why Christians should not see God at work in many cultures and religious traditions. Even those which at first look least sympathetic to belief in God, like Buddhism, have valuable insights to teach. The Buddhist tradition teaches that it may be unhelpful to be passionately attached to highly speculative doctrines, of which we have little objective certainty (like doctrines about the inner nature of God). Such attachment is especially unhelpful if it leads to intolerance and impatience with others. What is important, Buddhists say, is learning non-attachment to selfish desires and to the ego, learning to see the flow of events with inner calm and without grasping.

A Christian would probably wish to place much more stress on devotion to a personal Lord, and to the positive value of mediating the active love of God in practice (though in Buddhism there is in fact a great deal of devotional practice and social concern, too). Yet Christians can see a close analogy to their own way of salvation in the stress on non-attachment to possessions and to egoism, and on the goal of losing self in the ultimate experience of a state of wisdom, bliss and compassion (*nirvana*). For is God not a being of supreme wisdom, bliss and compassion, who is known by the renunciation of self? So, while Christians will continue to look to Jesus Christ as the source of their knowledge of God, there is no reason why Christians should not celebrate the Buddhist path as a true but different path to knowledge of God, inspired by God himself. Perhaps it is only when many different traditions learn to understand one another more fully that the fullness of that truth which is discerned in Christ will be revealed.

The Indian traditions, too, offer perspectives on God which can complement the Christian tradition, which has been so closely bound up with Byzantine and European culture. Indian traditions are enormously complex, but one theme that is found in the Upanishads, one of the main revealed scriptures of Hinduism, is the unity of all things in Brahman, the supreme reality. Whereas the European traditions have tended to see God as set over against the universe, and as quite different from it, the Upanishads teach that the supreme reality which has the nature of being, consciousness and bliss, is one with the universe, which is in a sense its temporal appearance. One Indian theologian, Ramanuja, calls the universe the 'body of the Supreme Lord', while another, Sankara, holds that all the distinct things we see in the universe are really illusory appearances of a reality which is in itself without distinctions or duality.

Again, at first sight this view of God, of the Supreme Reality, may seem very different from the Christian belief in a transcendent creator, who is quite distinct from all created beings. And I am not trying to suggest that all these views are in fact the same – of course, they are not. What is possible, however, is that the Upanishadic view arises from stressing the Divine immanence, the presence of the Lord within the heart, and within everything in the universe. After all, Christians believe that in Jesus, God entered into time, so the Christian God is not totally transcendent. Christians also believe that many people are called to be parts of the 'body of Christ' (the 'body of the Lord'), and even that the ultimate destiny of this universe is that all things should be united 'in Christ'.

So why could one not hold that God is both transcendent and immanent? That the Upanishads do record genuine experiences of God, apprehended at the heart of human selves, and within the things of the universe, while the Bible places more stress on the 'otherness' of God, as a morally commanding will? Here again, perhaps a deeper encounter of these traditions will bring out what is best in each, and remind each of aspects of the truth it has tended to overlook.

Christians are committed to thinking that at least one non-Christian religious tradition contains a genuine revelation of God. That is, of course, the ancient Hebrew faith recorded in the Hebrew Bible. Christians admittedly take a rather different view of that faith than do modern Jews, who interpret the Bible in terms of the Talmud and of Rabbinic teaching. Yet Christians are committed to believing that the Hebrew Bible, which they call the 'Old Testament', does truly reveal God, even if that revelation needs to be completed by appeal to the 'New Testament' revelation of God in Jesus. Indeed, the person of Jesus cannot be properly understood outside his Jewish background and culture. since he is seen as the fulfilment of promises made in the Old Testament.

Historical relations between Jews and Christians have not been happy, partly because some Christians have regarded Jews as people who rejected and killed the true Messiah. So for much of European history, Jews have been ostracised and penalised in various ways, a process culminating in the *Shoah*, or the attempted extermination of Jews in Nazi Germany under Hitler. It was not, of course, Christians who attempted that terrible course of genocide, and many Christians heroically opposed it. But it has to be admitted, with shame, that some Christian teaching about the Jews as rejectors of God and enemies of Christ, needing to be converted by force if necessary, prepared the way for attacks on Jews by the atheistic regime of Hitler.

Anti-Semitism has been an aspect of allegedly Christian societies throughout European history, and Christians need to come to terms with it and reject it openly and forcefully.

To do so one needs to come to a deeper understanding of Judaism, instead of relying on stereotypes which distort reality. The beginning of the Jewish way is also the beginning of the Christian way. It has, as its basis, the idea of a covenant or treaty made between God and the Patriarchs of the twelve nomadic tribes which combined to form the nation of Israel. God is said to have appeared, probably in dreams or visions, to Abraham, Isaac and Jacob, and to have promised divine protection in return for their obedience to divine law, the Torah (literally, the 'teaching' of God). These early prophets felt that God called them, and their descendants, into a special relationship with God, almost like a marriage, as some later prophets described it (see Hosea 2:16–20). God called them to a special vocation, which involved being true to God's law and being prepared to lead all people to the knowledge of God. At its highest, the covenant is a calling into a relationship of love with God, a relationship which is not meant to be kept for one's own people alone, but which is to be shared with the whole world.

This path is not one of world renunciation or conformity to sacred tradition. It is one which calls for the radical pursuit of justice and peace in a world filled with oppression and violence. In a sense, it is a revolutionary path, its adherents always urged on beyond their present understanding of things to see what real justice and mercy require. It is a path of hope, encouraging people to go on striving for justice, even when things might seem to be hopeless.

Because justice is something to be achieved in this world, there is a strong stress in the Hebrew faith on God as the liberator, or the one who raises up liberators ('saviours') to free his people from slavery and oppression. God is the one who saves his people from slavery in Egypt, from the wilderness, and from the militaristic empires which surround them. God raises up prophets, heroes and kings to lead his people to freedom. He promises them a homeland in which they can live in justice and peace, and in which they can enjoy the good things of creation, sharing them with all people. The reverse side of the liberating activity of God is divine judgement upon oppressors. The message of the prophets is that those who do evil will themselves be destroyed by evil, and that in the end all evil will be removed by God from creation. So judgement and liberation, justice and mercy, go together, though the prophets insist that it is the divine mercy which will triumph in the end, and that it is offered to all who truly repent, or turn from evil.

Many Jews have evoked the hope for a coming Messianic age, especially at times of trouble and distress. At the time of Jesus, there was more than one Messianic movement, which looked for a liberation of Israel from Roman rule, and the coming of a new age of justice and peace, in which Jews would play a leading role. Christians are those who accept that Jesus of Nazareth was the Messiah, but to do so they have to re-interpret much traditional Jewish expectation in a fairly radical way. For example, they have to accept that the Messiah will not inaugurate a new age of national liberation for Israel, and that somehow his death was of a significance rarely anticipated in the Hebrew Bible. The first Christians preached a message for the whole world, of a 'new Israel', the church, in which sins would be forgiven and in which a kingdom 'not of this world' would be promised to disciples. Many Jews – thousands, according to the New Testament – joined the new movement. All the apostles were Jews, and the message of Jesus' resurrection was first publicly preached in Jerusalem at the Jewish national festival of Pentecost. It is incorrect to say that 'the Jews' rejected Jesus, although it is true that those who did not accept the Messianic claims of Jesus largely remained loyal to their traditional faith.

It is not hard to see why many could not accept that Jesus was the Messiah. He was not, after all, a king from the royal house of David. He had been crucified as a criminal – and such a death was a standard refutation of claims to be a true prophet. He did not usher in a kingdom of peace and justice. Worst of all, his disciples quite soon gave up following Torah, so they left the revealed faith. When Christians began to worship Jesus as God, many Jews felt that their faith had been betrayed, and after the destruction of the Temple at Jerusalem, a new form of Judaism – Rabbinic Judaism – was formed, vowed to eternal loyalty to Torah.

So the tragic history of Jewish–Christian suspicion began. There are still many issues to be explored in Jewish–Christian relations today, but most accept that it is time for a new beginning, with greater understanding of one another's faith. The two faiths have an enormous amount in common. Christians accept that the prophets of Israel were men and women raised up by God to a new insight into the divine nature and purpose. The prophets give a distinctive witness to God's call for justice, they focus human attention squarely on this world and its problems, and they lead people to look to the future in hope for a fulfilment of God's purpose for the world. The Hebrew Bible records the lives and teachings of those prophets, and the story of the twelve tribes, as they pursued their tangled relationship to the God of their ancestor Abraham. Christians include this record in their own Bible, thus witnessing to God's covenant with his ancient people, the Jews, which will never be abolished.

So Christians can hold that Jesus is the expected Messiah, and that one day, whether in this world or the next, everyone, Jew and Gentile alike, will recognise that fact. But they can also hold that God calls whom he will into membership of the church, and it is not for us to question the motives either of those who follow Jesus or of those who are apparently not called to do so. They can also hold that God may will Jews, the people of the covenant, to continue loyal in their own path, until they have played their appointed role in human history. This seems to be the way Paul is thinking in the eleventh chapter of his letter to the Romans, and it enables Christians to give a much more positive place to Judaism in the religious history of the world, while remaining true to their own commitment to Jesus as Messiah.

The same sort of thing may be true of Islam, from a Christian point of view. Islam is a proselytising religion, and many Muslims would like to see the whole world living under the *Shari'a,* the law of God revealed in the Qur'an. Christianity shares with Islam a belief in one creator God who speaks through the prophets, and a belief in God's calling to a life of justice and honesty in this world, and to a life with God in Paradise after death. But Islam does not accept Jesus as the Son of God, or the Christian doctrines of the Trinity and of the atoning death of Jesus on the cross.

This has sometimes been seen in the past as a conscious rejection by Muslims of God's revelation in Jesus – and of course Muslims have often seen Christians as falling into idolatry by worshipping Jesus. There have been many misunderstandings on both sides, and it will take patience and sensitivity to clear them away. There is little reason to deny that Muslims have a revelation of God in the Qur'an, and that they do worship the same God that Christians do. Perhaps Christians can learn from Muslims much about the basic simplicity of faith in a creator, and about the possibility of direct 'mystical' experience of God. But Christians might well think that the knowledge of the redeeming love of God and of God's ultimate goal of uniting human and divine is shown in and through Jesus. Thus Christians can find good reason to co-operate in spiritual and moral projects with Muslims, while continuing to witness, in a non-coercive way, to the insight into the divine nature and goal that they believe themselves to have been given through Jesus of Nazareth.

It is not difficult, then, for Christians to see God at work everywhere, seeking to bring people to know the spiritual basis of the universe, and to liberate them from egoism and ignorance of spiritual reality. I have suggested that it is not too hard to see many religious traditions as preserving distinctive insights into the divine nature, which may be complementary to one another to a great extent.

## FIRST VIEW: ONLY CHRISTIANS CAN BE SAVED

There are, nevertheless, many differences between religious traditions, and some Christians would stress that the claims they make cannot be equally true. When Hinduism claims that human souls are reincarnated many times, that contradicts the Christian view that each human soul is newly created at birth. When Buddhism claims that there is no creator of the universe (or that, if there is, the fact is not religiously important), that contradicts the Christian view that God is the one and only creator of all things. When Islam claims that God has no son, Christians, even if they insist that the expression 'Son of God' is metaphorical, not literal, can hardly agree. To some people, these differences seem so great that one cannot say that all religions are equally acceptable. There must be one 'true religion', and if that religion defines what salvation is, then that is the only religion that can really lead to salvation.

So some Christians hold that Christianity is the only true religion. It is just true that Jesus is the son of God and the Saviour of the world. Salvation consists in accepting salvation through Jesus, and so, however much one might respect and even learn from other religions, in the end they cannot be vehicles of divine revelation and paths to salvation. Such a view has been held by Karl Barth, who denies that non-Christian religions are paths to salvation. He holds, however, that members of other faiths and human beings in general can be saved by Christ, even though they do not realise it. What he does not accept is that they are saved by means of the religion they profess. There are some Christians who hold that no one can be saved unless they explicitly profess belief in Jesus as Saviour. They would say that all humans are guilty of sin, and thus have no right to claim eternal life. It is the pure grace of God which steps in to redeem those whom God chooses, and no one has cause to complain that God's grace is limited. Rather, one should accept that the justice of God is absolutely fair, and give thanks that, nevertheless, some are plucked from destruction by a totally unmerited act of divine mercy.

## SECOND VIEW: ALL CAN BE SAVED, BUT ONLY BY JESUS CHRIST

Such a very restrictive view seems to most Christians to be incompatible with belief in a universally loving God. Most Christians prefer to accept the teaching of the second letter of Peter, and many other New Testament passages, that God does not wish 'that any should perish, but that all should reach repentance' (2 Peter 3:9). That will include that vast majority who have never heard of Jesus, let alone confessed him as Lord and Saviour. If God wants them to be saved, it follows that God must have done something to make it possible for them to be saved. Since the great religions claim to be paths of liberation from selfish desire, and towards experience of a being or state of wisdom, compassion and bliss, it is natural to suppose that God is working in those religious traditions to draw people closer to himself. For this view, non-Christian religions are paths of salvation, though they may contain beliefs which give inadequate or incorrect views about the nature of God and the way he is working his ultimate purpose out.

The best known theologian who takes such a view is the Roman Catholic theologian Karl Rahner, and it has been officially expressed in Roman Catholic documents from the second Vatican Council (especially *Gaudium et Spes,* 1965). God speaks to everyone in some way, and often speaks through their own religious traditions, so that saving grace is present to all people. However, this grace is usually not recognised – many people do not even believe in God – and many people can have no idea at all that there really is a gracious, compassionate God who is inviting them to eternal life. How God speaks to such people, we cannot say. Perhaps in the voice of conscience, perhaps through the beliefs and practices of their own very different religions, perhaps even through the presence of the poor and oppressed in their own societies.

There are many hidden voices and presences of God. But it is natural to hope that God will not always be wholly hidden, that he will make his nature and will known, and that people will be able to know that by which they are saved. This is perhaps the deepest meaning of the Biblical claim that Jesus came to fulfil the Law, to fulfil the prophetic anticipations of a closer, more inward knowledge of God. In him people could see what until then had been largely hidden. Seeing it, they could respond to God in a new and fuller way. The unknown God had become known and recognisable, and in consequence the path of salvation had become surer and clearer.

That is what God is doing in Jesus – not opening the only way to salvation to a few people for the first time, but opening the eyes of people to the true nature of the God who wills to save all, and thereby opening up a surer, clearer path to a salvation whose nature can be more truly understood than hitherto. The consequence is that people might well be encouraged to progress in their own faith. At the same time, however, one cannot disguise the belief that the Christian faith is in the end the true, more adequate faith, and that it is desirable that all people come to hold it, insofar as their consciences are enabled to do so by God.

## THIRD VIEW: ALL CAN BE SAVED BY THEIR OWN FAITH

For some Christians even this view is too restrictive, because it makes Christian faith in the end superior to all others. They would say that God saves people by many different paths, in many different faiths. There is no one surer, clearer path, but all ways can lead to God, if sincerely pursued. The Presbyterian theologian John Hick has argued strongly for such a view, calling it 'the Pluralistic hypothesis'. The Christian way of salvation is one among other ways of overcoming egoism and finding a transformation of self in relation to a higher reality of wisdom, compassion and bliss. Nevertheless, the Christian way does give a true insight into at least part of the infinite nature of God, who is seen as actively seeking to free humans from egoism and draw them into a loving relationship with the divine.

There are thus a number of ways of thinking about how God saves human beings. All Christians agree, however, that God saves humans by freeing them from the power of greed, hatred and despair, and placing them in a relation of love with the divine. They see God doing this in a decisive way in and through the life and death and resurrection of Jesus. But the saving action of God is not confined to the person of the historical Jesus. It spreads out from that point to extend to millions of people all over the world. There are disagreements about the best way to think of what God is doing in Jesus, and about how this action can be extended to the whole world. But the core of the Christian doctrine of salvation is that in the life of Jesus one can see what God is doing to deliver the human race from evil, and that by devotion to Jesus anyone can share in that salvation.

# 9 THE TRINITY

Christians believe that God is the creator of everything in the universe, of the whole of space–time. They share this belief with Jews, Muslims, many Hindus and other religious believers. But Christians also have a quite distinctive belief about God which others often find hard to understand. The Christian God is a Trinity, a threefold God, a God who is described as 'Father, Son and Holy Spirit'.

It is easy to see how this description arose. Jesus was revered by his disciples as one who brought God close to them, whose presence mediated the presence of God, and whose actions seemed to express the love of God. After his resurrection, he was believed to have been vindicated by God as more than a prophet or teacher, more even than the Messianic king. He was seen to be the very image of God in human history, one whose humanity expressed and mediated the divine life itself.

It may seem that we could simply say that Jesus was God incarnate on earth. But Jesus prayed to God as his Father. In the Garden of Gethsemane, he prayed that his Father's will, and not his will, should be done (Luke 22:42). In John's gospel, he says that his Father lives in him, and he lives in the Father (John 14:10). Yet he does not just identify himself with his Father. So the prologue to John's gospel says that the Word (or Son) was *with* the Father from the beginning (John

1:1–3). The Word became flesh and suffered death as a man, but the Father remained the almighty ruler of heaven and earth.

Moreover, Jesus promised that his Father would send a 'Paraclete' (or advocate), one who would be with humans as their advocate and support, who would give them an inner joy, hope and love (John 14:16, 17). Indeed, the Christian church could be said to have come into being at Pentecost, when the Holy Spirit descended upon the disciples in what seemed to them like 'tongues of fire' (Acts 2:1–4). God is present in the hearts of human beings, not as the all-creating Father nor as the eternal Word, but as the life-giving Spirit who shapes humans in the image of the Word and unites them in love to the Father.

It took more than a century before the early Christians came to work out what their new faith in Jesus as the Christ implied about God. As they prayed and reflected, they became more certain that what the divine revelation in Jesus showed was the threefold form of God. The Father who created the universe, the Son who became incarnate and died to liberate humans from the power of sin, and the Spirit who brought the divine love itself into human hearts and minds, were all ways in which God himself existed.

Early theologians had great difficulty in finding an exact formulation of this belief. There were many different suggestions, and the one they eventually decided upon was never felt to be wholly satisfactory. As Augustine once said, it was only that it was better than saying nothing. The formula they arrived at was that God is 'three persons in one substance'. But that formula needs some explaining, before we can see what it means.

The word 'person' is a translation of the Latin 'persona', and of the Greek 'hypostasis'. The problem is that it has a range of possible meanings. At one end, it can mean the mask that an actor wore in a drama, giving the idea of a role or part that one can play for a while. At the other end, it means something like a 'thing' or individual, which can be identified and distinguished from other individuals.

Just to complicate matters even further, the word 'substance' also has a range of possible meanings. It translates the Latin 'substantia' and the Greek 'ousia' (most of the early Christian doctrines were formulated in Greek, and translated into Latin in the Western church). At one end, it means a kind of stuff, like 'gold' or 'hydrogen'. So you can ask, 'What kind of a substance is this?', meaning 'What kind of stuff is it made of?' At the other end, it means an individual which exists by its own power, independently of anything else. In that sense, perhaps there is only one substance, which would be God. For only God exists without being dependent on anything else for its existence.

It is obvious that there can be quite a large range of interpretations of what the Trinity is, depending on which meaning of these two words, 'person' and 'substance', one accepts. I shall mention just three main interpretations, which have been quite widely accepted by significant groups of Christians.

## FIRST VIEW: THE SOCIAL TRINITY

One interpretation is that 'persons' are individuals, and indeed individuals with consciousness and will. This is very like the ordinary English use of the word 'person', to refer to an individual agent with reason and will. The word 'substance' can then be interpreted to mean 'kind of thing'. One can say that there are three centres of consciousness and will which together make up one kind of being, the divine being, God. To say there are three persons in one substance is then to say that there are three rational agents of the same kind, which together are called 'God'. It is important to see that there are no other agents of that kind, and that those three agents are linked together in such a way that they cannot ever exist apart.

Father, Son and Spirit are like three minds linked together in a total harmony of consciousness and will. They always act together, and are each involved in a distinctive way in every divine action. Thus in creation the Father creates the universe through the Son and in the power of the Spirit. On the cross the Father liberates humanity through the self-giving action of the Son and by the life-giving power of the Spirit. At the end of time the Father will draw all things to himself through the Son and by the reconciling and unifying power of the Spirit.

In each case one of the divine persons seems to play a more significant or obvious role – the Father creates, the Son redeems and the Spirit unites all things to God. Yet in fact all three are acting together at all times, the role of each being a necessary part of the complete action of the divine being. The Father could not create without the wisdom of the Son and the creative energy of the Spirit. The Son could not redeem without the vindicating action of the Father and the inward action of the Spirit. The Spirit could not unite to the divine without the power of the Father and the pattern of the divine Wisdom that is found on earth in Jesus.

On this interpretation, there is not in fact one cosmic mind sustaining the universe. 'God' is a social or communal reality, consisting of three cosmic minds, always acting together, bound together by what has been called 'perichoresis' – a sort of mutual indwelling of each with the others. This view of the Trinity is most characteristic of the Eastern Orthodox churches, having been held by Gregory of Nyssa and other Cappadocian (Turkish) theologians. In recent times it has become widely held in the West, too, and modern exponents are John Zizioulas and Richard Swinburne.

The idea that God is a community of persons can be very surprising to monotheists, and Jews and Muslims often react strongly against it. But Christians who take this interpretation insist that they do not believe in three gods. There are not three divine beings who might argue or conflict with one another, like the Greek and Roman gods. It is the three persons together who make up the one and only God. 'God' is the name for that unity, which is a unity of love. The three persons are bound together in mutual love, and because of that Christians can truly say that 'God is love' (1 John 4:8).

The way this is sometimes put is to say that the Father is the source or cause of the other two 'persons'. Because love is inherently self-giving, the Father wills to share his being with another. He forms a perfect image of himself in the Son, each giving and receiving love from the other in perfect unity of being and will. Because love is something which is shared and bears fruit, Father and Son share their love with the Spirit, and the three are bound together in the most intimate form of union, a union of perfect and indestructible love. Thus the divine being is in itself a complete and perfect communion of love. However difficult and abstruse the doctrine of the Trinity may sometimes seem, it is basically a simple matter of saying that the one supreme God consists of a threefold communion of given, received and shared love. That, it would be said, is the highest form of value that there can possibly be, and so it is deeply appropriate that it should be found within the very being of God.

It might be said that if one insists too much on an absolute unity or oneness in God, that allows for no diversity or complexity, no relationship or mutuality in the divine being. Whereas a Trinitarian God includes diversity and relationship within an overarching unity of being. This helps one to see the supreme reality upon which the whole universe is formed as a reality which exemplifies perfect love. It is therefore a good model for a universe in which diversity, relationship and self-giving love are important values, which can be founded in the divine being itself.

## SECOND VIEW: THREE WAYS OF BEING GOD

In the main Western tradition a rather different interpretation of the Trinity has been more common. In the West a greater emphasis has been placed on the unity of the divine being. Most Western theologians have said that there is only one centre of consciousness and will in God, not three. True, there are three 'persons' in one 'substance', but the term person should not be understood as an individual rational agent, with its own independent will. Rather, it should be understood as an aspect or mode of being in which God exists. The one omnipotent and omniscient individual who is God exists in three distinct modes of being. For this view, the word 'person' in its modern

English sense is very misleading, and it should be understood as a 'way of being', not as a separate individual agent. Theologians who take this sort of view include Thomas Aquinas and, in recent times, Karl Barth and Karl Rahner.

When Christians speak of the Father, they speak of the primal source of all being, the creator of the universe, who always remains completely transcendent or above all created beings. That is one way in which God exists, as the transcendent source of all beings. The term 'Father' is a metaphor which tradition has taken to be appropriate to refer to the transcendent creator and sustainer of all things.

When Christians speak of the Son, they speak of the eternal Wisdom of God, who becomes incarnate as a man to liberate humans from hatred, greed and destruction. This is one and the same God as the Father, but it is not God considered as transcendent and always distinct from creation. It is God in a different aspect, as entering into creation, as uniting finite and infinite in the divine being.

Most classical Western theologians have insisted that God is eternal or timeless. Because God is absolutely perfect, God cannot change either for better or for worse. Nothing can affect God for the worse, and nothing can make God better than he is. So God is completely changeless in perfection, in power, bliss and knowledge. So when they say that God the Son becomes incarnate, they do not mean that God changes to become a man. They mean that the changeless God unites, and has eternally willed to unite, human nature to the divine nature in Jesus. It is the human which is raised up to share in the divine life, not the divine which comes down to a human level.

It is in this uniting and liberating action that God the Son differs from God the Father. It is the same God who is the transcendent creator and the liberating Saviour. Yet these are distinct activities of the divine being, different ways in which the one God exists and acts. So one can speak of there being different modes of divine experiencing and acting, even though there is only one omnipotent, omniscient God.

In a similar way, the Holy Spirit is God seen as acting within the lives and consciousnesses of created persons to complete the work of the Son by uniting all faithful human persons positively to the divine, as Jesus was united to the divine in a unique way. Indeed, the Spirit works to unite all creation to God, and unite all things in Christ. As the Son assumed human nature to God in Jesus, so the Spirit unites all created being to God, following the pattern established in the life of Jesus.

The threefold God is transcendent creator, liberating Saviour, and the Spirit immanent in all things uniting them to the divine life. It is rather as if one person can operate in three different modes. We might think of one person with three different personalities. That would be quite inadequate if we took it too literally, since God cannot be thought of as a split personality. But it might give the idea of how the one personal reality of God can exist and operate in quite different forms of being – as the wholly ineffable source of all being, as the glorious Lord who liberates the world and reigns as king in the redeemed community, and as the immanent Spirit present in all things to unite them to the divine.

These are not three different beings, not even three individual and different agents. They are not three 'persons' of the same sort who can relate to one another in mutual love. So this view differs from the 'social Trinity' view. They are three different forms in which the one God exists. But those forms of being are not temporary, arbitrary or accidental forms of God. They are all essentially parts of what God is. So on this view a Trinitarian view of God would see God not as a bare undifferentiated unity (the Father), not as one personal cosmic Mind (the Son), and not as the immanent spiritual energy including and active in all finite things (the Spirit), but as one reality who exists in these three forms of being, and who can only be properly understood when all three aspects are held together.

Both these interpretations of the Trinity have been combined with the belief that God is essentially timeless, perfect, and so does not change in any way (is immutable), and is not affected by what happens in the world in any way (is impassible). We might think of the whole of time, from the first moment to the last, as spread out along a line. God is not anywhere on that line, but is outside it, and brings it all into being in one creative act, without changing. So God creates the last moment of time in the very same 'eternal act' in which he creates the first moment of time, and all the other moments too.

That means the incarnation is not a new idea of God's. God thinks of, and brings about, the union of the man Jesus with the eternal Son in the very same act as he creates the Big Bang with which the universe began. It means that the Holy Spirit is not really doing one thing after another in time, though it seems so to us. Rather, in the one act of creation, God the Spirit unites the universe to the divine life. Creation and redemption are the same act so far as God is concerned.

God does not have to wait and see what happens in the universe before he decides how to respond. For God brings everything about in one act, and it just seems to us that events unfold in time towards an unknown future. The future is not unknown to God. He knows it perfectly, as equally present with what is to us the past and the present. On both these views of God, then, the history of the universe adds nothing to the changeless being of God. Rather, God is the unchanging reality which the whole universe derives from, strives to imitate, and will eventually be united to, when all evil has been eliminated from finite beings. Whether God is a loving communion of persons or one omnipotent, omniscient being in three different forms of existence, the Trinity is a reality eternally complete in itself, and the whole finite cosmos is only a faint image of its glory, and shares, by grace, in a tiny part of its perfect life.

Both these interpretations of the Trinity have a long history in Christian theology, and they are typical of Eastern and Western forms of Christian theology, respectively. Both of them tend to think of the Trinity in its own esssential being (what is called 'the immanent Trinity'), as opposed to thinking of it in relation to the created universe ('the economic Trinity'). They are reflective ways of trying to work out and understand what is involved in the threefold nature of God, as that is suggested in the New Testament witness to God as

Father, as somehow present in Jesus, and as experienced in the power of the Holy Spirit. But they move a long way beyond the New Testament, and to some they seem to move too far, in claiming to explain what God is like in his innermost being. They also seem to remove God from any real relation to time and to the things and persons in time. Perhaps, some will say, all we can know is what God has revealed of himself in Christ and in the Church, and perhaps God is changed by the events of the Cross and the creative activity of the Spirit. The innermost secrets of the divine being may remain hidden in the cloud of unknowing which must forever veil the divine source of all being. Of course what God reveals of himself must be true, but maybe it is enough to say that it is true in relation to us and our understanding, without penetrating into the divine nature itself.

## THIRD VIEW: THE HISTORY OF THE THREEFOLD GOD

So there is a third way of approaching the doctrine of the Trinity. We could see the Trinity as a way of thinking about God as he relates to us in revelation and salvation, as a way of understanding how God really acts in time, in new and creative ways, to bring about human liberation. In this relation of God to time, there are three main phases of the divine creative activity.

The first phase of the divine activity is that by which God generates the universe by his primordial creative will. Out of the infinity of the divine being God generates the whole set of possible beings, in their endless diversity. Among these possibilities, there are some that are uncreatable, since in them the powers of destruction outweigh the powers of creativity. But there may still be countless numbers of possible universes in which various sorts of unique goodness and value can exist, which could not exist in just that way in any other universe. From that huge set of possibilities, God selects (at least) one set for its creative possibilities, and brings it into actuality by generating this physical universe.

This creative activity of God itself has a threefold aspect. There is God in his transcendent infinity ('the Father'), God in his all-conceiving wisdom, thinking of all possible universes ('the Son'), and God in the energy of creative actualisation ('the Spirit'). The Father can be seen as the ultimate underived source of all being. The Son is the pattern or archetype of created being, through whom all things are created, and as images of whom they exist. The Spirit is the life-giving power who gives existence and independence to created beings, and urges them to begin their long journey towards conscious, creative and responsive personal life.

This view of God is expressed in the New Testament, particularly in the first chapter of the letters to the Colossians and to the Ephesians. In the letter to the Colossians Christ (the eternal Son) is described as 'the image of the invisible God', in whom 'all things were created', and in whom 'all things hold together' (Colossians 1:13–17). He gives name and form to what remains always invisible in the being of the Father, and the whole universe is held together as one in him. It is obvious that the writer is not referring just to the earthly Jesus, even though he sees Jesus as the embodiment on earth of this cosmic Christ. Christ is the archetype of the cosmos, and the Spirit is the power which gives this archetype existence and vitality.

The second phase of divine creativity activity is the continuing relation of God to the physical cosmos, as it develops from the initial Big Bang to forms of individual complex existence which become aware of themselves and their environment. With regard to the physical cosmos, with its millions of galaxies and planetary systems, God remains always transcendent, infinitely far beyond them in reality and power. Yet God, out of his measureless infinity, also relates to conscious creatures. On the planet earth God does so in a very particular way. Jesus, because of his unique unity with the cosmic Christ, becomes the expression and vehicle of the eternal Son, the image of God in human history, the historical form of the eternal Son. He relates to the transcendent aspect of God as to a Father, the intimately known sustainer of his existence. His relation to the Father is one of both difference and unity. It is one of difference, because the eternal Wisdom, united to a particular human nature, is to be distinguished from the utterly transcendent and infinite source of all being. It is one of unity, because it is the same God, existing under different aspects, who is both infinite source and incarnate Wisdom.

The human being Jesus relates to God in a threefold way. He reveres the self-existence of God the Father, upon whom his existence wholly depends. He expresses in his own person the wisdom of God the Son. And he mediates the creative power of God the Spirit. In actualising that threefold relationship to the divine he presents the exemplary pattern on earth of created personal life, the pattern which at its best is to be actualised in all created persons. All created persons should revere the Father as self-existent source of all being, express in their own lives the being of the Son as a historical actualisation of self-giving, transforming love, and mediate the creative power of the Spirit. Jesus is the exemplar of created personal being because he actualises this threefold relationship perfectly and in an unconditional way. For the rest of us, that exemplary pattern remains an ideal which we only fitfully and partially approach. And we do so only inasmuch as the Spirit acts in us to enable us to grow into the image of the Son, who is the perfect historical image of the invisible God.

In Jesus, God the Son enters into human history, giving up his life of perfect bliss so that he can share in the sorrows of humanity, and lead humans into a broader and fuller life of unity with God. The archetype of all creation becomes the historical exemplar of the divine mind and will. When Jesus dies, it is the Holy Spirit who carries on the work of the Incarnation, bringing the presence of Christ into the hearts of millions who have never met the historical Jesus. The Spirit makes the life of Christ a present power in the lives of all those who respond in faith.

So the second phase of the divine activity in creation is the entry of the divine into the flux of history, so that humans can be delivered from egoism and united to God in love. God, who has given creatures a measure of freedom, does not leave them without a guide, even when they have rejected the way of virtue. God at all times seeks to

inspire, to attract, to co-operate with, and to respond to human decisions. Sometimes this response must be in judgement, to prevent the
harms that humans do from destroying the divine purpose itself. But
it is also always in love, seeking the ultimate good of every creature
in due measure.

So humans can rightly respond to God as a Father, who wills their
well-being, as the Son Incarnate in Jesus, who gives up his freedom
from suffering to share the sorrows of earthly life for their sake, and
as the life-giving Spirit, who sows in their lives the seeds of joy, compassion, patience and wisdom insofar as they learn to rely solely on
God. The threefold God enters into the human story in continuing
inspiration and response, to lead them towards the goal implicit in
the first moment of creation. For this interpretation of the Trinity,
God truly enters into time, expressing the divine being in new and
creative ways, responding to the acts of creatures, and co-operating
with them in forwarding the divine purpose of realising new forms of
being and value in a created community of persons.

The third phase of divine creative activity is the reception of the
whole temporal history of the universe into the divine consciousness.
Having generated the cosmos in freedom, and related to it with self-
giving and co-operative love, God embraces all its completed values,
as a new determination of the divine being. In this respect, it is the
Spirit who gathers up all the scattered fragments of created finite
awareness and unites them in one integrated divine experience. The
work of the Spirit is to eliminate evil and suffering from creation, and
bring the values generated by creatures to fulfilment. The Spirit
works throughout the cosmos to guide it towards its proper perfection. The goal is that conflict and destruction should be overcome,
and a community of compassion and contemplative delight should
come into being – the kingdom of God.

In that community, the Christ who was in Jesus will be fully
expressed and active in the lives of all personal beings, who will form
the 'body of Christ', the social, historical vehicle of the creative will
and consciousness of God. As Christ was the archetype of created

being, and the historical exemplar of personal being on earth in the person of Jesus, so he is to be the pleroma of created being, the fulness of social and personal existence, expressed in a community of persons related in love.

At that point, which may only be possible in a new form of creation, all created persons will rejoice in co-operating freely to form a communal expression of the cosmic Christ. The whole of created being will be united in Christ, fulfilling God's purpose 'to unite all things in him, things in heaven and things on earth' (Ephesians 1:10). When Christians talk of the 'return of Christ in glory', they are on this view using symbols to think of this fulfilment of all creation in a truly personal community, which is fully responsive to and therefore expressive of the creative will of God.

God is not only the creator and sustainer of this community. God is also the one who receives all finite experiences into his own all-embracing experience, and rejoices in the final beauty and goodness of creation. So the community who form the body of the pleromal Christ offer up their experiences to God, who accepts them into the divine being, and there transforms them into moments of unfading beauty and joy by their inclusion in the divine infinity. As all things come from God the Father, so finally all things return to him. In the divine mind, every moment of created goodness is present imperishably and indestructibly.

On this interpretation of God's Trinitarian life, which can be found in some form in a number of recent theologians like John Macquarrie and Catherine Lacugna, the threefold nature of God is expressed in the cosmic process of creation, co-operation and consummation. God creates the universe in the power of the Spirit and on the pattern of the Son, in order to generate communities of finite personal agents. God co-operates with those communities by the inspiring and guiding power of the Spirit, whose nature is fully expressed and actualised on earth in the person of Jesus, the incarnate Son, to liberate them from hatred, greed and egoism. God consummates the universe by the integrating and reconciling power of the Spirit, seeking to include all creation in the 'body', the historical and social form of the Son, and to preserve all created values in the divine awareness for ever.

The Trinitarian action of God is, on this view, an essentially temporal, social action. The love of God is not something internal to the Trinity in itself, perfectly complete apart from creation. It is worked out in relation to created persons in a finite universe, with all the risk and pain that inevitably involves. The universe itself is part of the history of God, and to speak of the Trinity is to speak of the ways in which the divine being is expressed by creating and relating to what is other than itself, and in which the universe is united to the divine life by the self-giving and co-operating love of God. God enters into the finite and temporal in order that the finite and temporal might be united to the infinite life of eternity. That is the final mystery of Christian revelation, and what distinguishes Christian belief in God from forms of monotheism which insist that God and creation must always remain separate.

The doctrine of the Trinity may sound rather complicated – but it is not after all surprising that human attempts to understand God should stretch the human mind as far as it can go. Despite these crude and faltering attempts to comprehend the threefold nature of God, it should not be forgotten that the idea of the Trinity is basically very simple. Christians worship God as the creator of the universe, always beyond and greater than the whole of creation. Christians worship God as one who enters into the universe, especially in the person of Jesus, to liberate persons from hatred and greed, and lead them to eternal life. Christians worship God as the Spirit who inspires, guides and strengthens the hearts and minds of created persons, and brings them into the closest loving union with God.

God the sustainer of all creation, God revealed and known in the person of Jesus, and God active within human minds and hearts – all these are forms of the one true God. So Christians worship the one God who is known in many different ways and approached by many different paths. But because of what they believe to be his self-revelation in Jesus, they claim to know him as the threefold God, who wishes to bring all created persons to know and delight in his love for ever. Whatever their interpretations of the Trinity, these are the fundamental beliefs about God that all Christians share.

# 10 THE CHURCH

For most people, Christianity is not some sort of abstruse theological system. They come across it as embodied in a particular set of social institutions, the churches. People might love or hate the churches, but they are distinctive communities which have a strong personal and social impact on human lives. Why should there be churches, and not just groups of people meeting to discuss matters of common spiritual interest? There are many people who would say they are reasonably good people, even Christian people, but who are not members of any church. Why should the church be important?

The basic reason is to do with the Christian perception of God's purpose for creation, and God's actions in human history to achieve that purpose. Christians see God's purpose as being to develop communities of creativity and contemplation. Human persons are to find their fulfilment, not in isolation, but in co-operating with one another in many creative enterprises, in helping one another in trouble, and in sharing in the understanding and appreciation of the good things of creation. So if religion is about human fulfilment in relation to God, the supreme spiritual reality, it is necessarily about the building-up of healthy, creative communities.

The fact is, however, that human beings have largely turned away from this divine purpose, and now find themselves trapped by selfish egoism, hatred of others, and the pursuit of pleasure at the expense of goodness. Christians believe that God's response to this situation is to create a 'counter-cultural community', a society which will try to counter the forces of egoism and hatred, and encourage the pursuit of creative excellence, universal compassion and worthwhile happiness.

The twelve tribes of Israel were called by God as a 'covenant community', a people who would be wholly devoted to God, and who would be God's instrument to bring the 'fallen' world back to the divine plan. The covenant was that God would remain faithful to his promise to bring the world to fulfilment through Israel, as long as Israel remained true to the divine teaching, the Torah, which was to be the means of keeping them in union with God.

From a Christian point of view, it may be held that this covenant will always remain in force. Yet Christians believe that God also made a new covenant in and through the person of Jesus, bringing a new covenant community into being. This new community is the church, again a people called to be devoted to God and to reconcile the world to God. What is new about it is that it is not confined to one nation, but is open to all people of every race and nation. And it does not have one special set of divinely given laws, but is promised the inner power of the Spirit of Christ to unite its members inwardly to God. So the church is the community of the new covenant given by God through Jesus, and maintained by the living power of the Spirit.

To be a Christian is to accept membership of this community of the Spirit, and in this sense one simply cannot be a Christian and not be a member of the church. The church is not some sort of voluntary association of like-minded people. It is a particular community called by God to reconcile the world to God, and it will include people of the most diverse kinds and characters. Moreover, the church is to make present in every age and place the self-giving, reconciling action of the eternal Christ. It is to reproduce in its life the divine life which was fully present in Jesus. It is to 'die' with him in renouncing selfish desire. It is to 'rise' with him, in bringing the victorious life of the Spirit into the world.

Christians are agreed that the church is the means by which the reconciling presence and activity of God is actualised in the world, so that the church should seek to extend its divinely given proclamation to every part of the world. Yet there are differing interpretations of just what the church is and ought to be. For that reason there are many different churches, which represent different particular ways of trying to realise communities of the Spirit of Christ in the world.

## FIRST VIEW: THE CHURCH AS A SACRAMENTAL COMMUNITY

One major view is that represented by the Roman Catholic Church, the largest Christian denomination. Since the church is the body of Christ (1 Corinthians 12:27), and is meant to be an agent of divine reconciliation, the church should be visibly united. One cannot have a divided church, and so there must be a visible symbol and guarantee of the church's unity. That is the Pope, the Bishop of Rome, who is by tradition the successor of Peter (*Petrus*), of whom Jesus said that he (or his declaration that Jesus was the Christ) would be the rock (*Petra*) on whom the church would be founded (Matthew 16:18).

The Roman Catholic doctrine of the Papacy has developed considerably over the centuries, but the view now is that the Pope is the chief pastor and teacher of the whole church. He is protected from error (i.e. is infallible) when solemnly defining any matter of faith and morals, and no authentic decision of the church on such matters can be made without him. He is the Vicar of Christ, and ultimately all authority in the church flows from him, as the representative of Christ on earth.

The Pope nevertheless does not usually define matters of faith on his own, but convenes ecumenical (worldwide) Councils of Bishops, who are the successors of the twelve apostles, and whose decisions, when understood to be ratified by the Pope, are binding on the whole church. The bishops guarantee that the church is truly 'apostolic', that is, validly descended by the imposition of hands from the first apostles, and so the church can be trusted to continue and develop the apostolic teaching, derived from Jesus himself.

On the Roman Catholic view, the church has a teaching authority (a *magisterium*), given by God, to preserve and amplify the teaching which God gave in Jesus, and faithful Catholics have a duty to accept this teaching as having divine authority. Nevertheless, this is not in practice the most important aspect of the life of the Catholic Church. For most Catholics, it is the sacramental life of the church which counts most. By baptism, in which water is usually poured on the forehead of a child in the name of the Trinity, God receives children into the redeemed community, and purifies them of the guilt of original sin. In confirmation, when the Bishop lays his hands on the heads of candidates, God gives the grace of the Holy Spirit to help one in the practice of the Christian life. In marriage, by their mutual vows and by the blessing of a priest, couples are joined by God into a union of 'one flesh'. In confession, the priest has authority to declare the sins of the faithful forgiven. In unction, by anointing with oil and prayer, the soul is prepared for death. In ordination, by the laying on of hands, priests are set apart to offer the sacrifice of the Mass. And most importantly, in the Mass bread and wine are transformed by the words of priestly consecration (repeating the words of Jesus, 'This is my body ... this is my blood') into the body and blood of Christ, who offers the sacrifice of his own life to atone for the sins of the faithful, and as they receive the consecrated bread and wine he places his own eternal life within them.

In all these ways, through the authorised hierarchy of bishops and priests, the grace of God is conveyed by material means – water, wine, oil and bread – to cleanse the soul from sin and unite it to God. The sacramental principle is that matter becomes the expression and vehicle of the divine presence and power, which flows from the person of Jesus, through the priestly ministry of the church, to the whole world. The sacraments in a real sense continue the Incarnation, as the Spirit takes 'flesh', or material form in history. This is especially true in the Mass, when bread and wine, symbols of human work and suffering, become the very presence of Christ among his people. As the priest offers the bread and wine to God, he does so in the person of

Christ, who is truly present, offering the sacrifice of himself so that the faithful may be released from the penalty of sin and brought near to God. Each Mass is a real propitiatory sacrifice, in which sins are forgiven and the grace of God is given to sanctify, or make holy, human lives.

In the sacraments, the church makes the eternal Christ present, just as he was in Jesus, makes the material an expression and vehicle of the spiritual, and takes Jesus' work of forgiving, reconciling and uniting to God throughout the world, until the end of human history. In traditional Catholic thought, the church is the 'ark of salvation', and all must enter into it to be saved, or freed from sin and united to God. Yet it has almost always been taught that all humans can be saved, even if they are not Catholics, as long as it can plausibly be said that they would have joined the church, had they understood it adequately.

Orthodox Christians share most of the Roman Catholic vision of the church as the ark of salvation, the sacramental community which is meant to bring God's grace to all people, and the guardian of the truths of faith and morals which God has confirmed or revealed in Jesus Christ. They do not accept, however, that the Pope is the head of the whole church, maintaining that only the bishops meeting together in ecumenical councils can speak for the church in matters of faith and morals. In practice, the Orthodox churches exist as largely national (e.g. Russian or Greek) churches, under their own Patriarchs, or chief bishops. They regard the Bishop of Rome as just one of the ancient Patriarchs, along with Constantinople and others, even if he is granted a certain pre-eminence of honour. They maintain that no truly ecumenical (worldwide) council has met since the second council of Nicaea, in 787 (the seventh ecumenical council), before the division of the church between East and West. So they tend to see the Roman Catholic Church as introducing new and unacceptable doctrines of church authority, which overthrow the most ancient traditions of the equality and collegiality of all bishops under God.

## SECOND VIEW: THE CHURCH AS A FELLOWSHIP OF FAITH

Since the sixteenth century a great number of churches have sprung up which 'protest' against various Roman Catholic doctrines and practices, and so are generally called Protestant churches. They have usually claimed to return to a purer and more primitive Christian faith, in the face of what they saw as widespread corruption and superstition; but because they have left the institutional unity of the Roman Catholic church, they have had to develop a rather different doctrine of the church.

The main development is to regard the church not as a visible institution, but as an invisible, spiritual unity, whose true extent and membership is known only to God. The invisible church is made up of all those who are truly disciples of Jesus Christ, who worship him as their Lord and Saviour. There is no other head of the church except Jesus, and there is no need of any priestly hierarchy to mediate between Jesus and the believer.

Of course Christians are called to form communities in which worship can be offered to God, and in which the Christian virtues of sharing and loving fellowship can be practised. But these may be local communities, perhaps bound in loose federations, either national or in terms of a core of shared beliefs or practices, but having no centralised hierarchical structure. Indeed, ministers are often called by local congregations to serve them, on the New Testament principle that those who would truly follow Christ are called to serve, not to tell others what to do. All these local communities, or at least those of their members who are truly devoted to Christ, form the invisible church, the body of Christ, called to be conformed to his image and to do his work in the world.

The institutional church as such has no absolute authority in faith and morals, and it is usually held that all church councils can fall into error, however ecumenical they are. There is usually a great concern to maintain the true apostolic faith. But this is held to reside, not in a body of people supposed to be descended from the apostles by ordination, but in the Bible, which preserves the original apostolic witness in a pure and uncorrupted form. For most Protestants, the Bible alone is the source and test of all religious and moral beliefs.

For some Protestants, human reason has been corrupted by sin, and so one cannot have a 'natural theology', which can argue to God without the aid of revelation, or a 'natural law' in morality, which can be apprehended by reason, without appeal to revelation. The Bible is the only means of access to divine truth. By it all particular churches must be judged, and by it they all must live. So in Protestant churches the pulpit, where the Bible is read and commented on, is often more prominent than the altar, which indeed becomes a 'holy table' around which the Lord's Supper is celebrated, perhaps once a month.

It is agreed that the church should not be divided. But giving local churches autonomy is not seen as division, and is regarded as being entirely compatible with the deepest spiritual unity. The true test of unity is not the acceptance of some common human leader, but acceptance of the central teachings of the Bible. Regrettably, perhaps, the interpretation of the Bible is not agreed by all Christians. So from the first there have been different varieties of Protestants, stressing different elements of Biblical teaching. Most Protestant churches do not see themselves as sacramental communities, mediating divine grace through priestly rituals. They do have sacraments, usually holding that there are only two sacraments ordained by Jesus – baptism and the Lord's Supper. There are many different interpretations of these sacraments, but on the whole it is denied that they convey divine grace just by their performance (*ex opere operato*). Baptism, sometimes limited to adults and, in Baptist churches by total immersion in water, may be seen as the public profession of faith in Christ. The Lord's Supper is usually not seen as any sort of propitiatory sacrifice, but as a memorial of Jesus' death for human sins, and a thanksgiving for redemption.

The crucial belief is that entrance into the local fellowship of the church is by the personal profession of faith (the conscious, willing acceptance of God's gift of grace). Redemption is given by God's free grace, and accepted in personal faith, so no outward ceremony or ritual is necessary, and undergoing such rituals will not by itself effect salvation. Nevertheless, immersion in the water of baptism, and sharing bread and wine in the Lord's Supper, are fitting symbols and public professions of the believer's personal commitment, and the acceptance of the life of Christ into one's own life.

It is important to most Protestants that the church should not be seen as a mediator between the individual and God. The church is made up of fallible and sinful people, and in its visible form it consists of millions of local fellowships of those who gather together to hear God's word in the Bible, deepen personal faith in the saving work of Jesus Christ, and proclaim the good news of salvation to the world. The church is the fellowship of people of faith. It consequently exists in a great variety of forms and local practices, always and everywhere seeking only to guide its life by Biblical teaching. The church is not a divinely appointed mediator of divine grace to the world, and no human committee of church people is an infallible teacher of faith and morals.

So there is an emphasis in Protestant Christianity on the right and duty of all believers to participate in the organisation of their own Christian fellowship. Protestants are generally averse to having a special class of priests, or of monks and nuns, who are called to devote their lives to God in a higher way. Everyone is called to the devout life, and to live it out by earning a living in the secular world. Thus there are no specially designated 'saints', who have lived lives of heroic virtue. All people are saved by grace, by a free gift of God which cannot be earned, and one cannot divide Christians into first-class and second-class citizens. The church has no authority to designate some people as saints, to release anyone from the punishments of Purgatory, or to lay down conditions (penances) for obtaining divine forgiveness. All these things are given solely at the good pleasure of God. The 'power of the keys', which Christ gave first to Peter (Matthew 16:19) and later to all the apostles (Matthew 18:18), is the power to declare the gospel of God's forgiveness, and thereby to open the doors of salvation to all. It is not the power to lay down humanly invented conditions of salvation. The church, for Protestants, simply does not have that sort of authority, which belongs only to God.

It would be quite wrong, however, to think that the doctrine of the church is unimportant to Protestants. On the contrary, the idea of the church as the invisible or hidden body of Christ in the world is a powerful one, stressing that true unity is inward and spiritual, not institutional. And the idea of the *koinonia*, of a loving fellowship in which joys and sorrows can be shared, and in which disciples can and should encourage one another in their personal devotion to Christ, is an essential part of the Protestant faith. Personhood is essentially social, and to be a disciple of Christ is necessarily to live in a community in which can be realised the gifts and fruits of the Spirit of Christ. But such communities grow from the 'bottom up', as people of faith come together to help each other grow in understanding of the Biblical promise of new life in Christ.

The church is for Protestants always the product of personal faith. Its teachings must always be subordinate to the Biblical revelation, and its practices must always be judged by whether or not they build up the fruits of the Spirit – of joy, patience, peace, faith and hope (Galatians 5:22) – in the hearts of believers. This is clearly a very different picture of the church from the traditional Catholic picture of a priestly, authoritative, centralised and sacramental institution, so much so that some people have regarded Catholicism and Protestantism as different religions. However, they share the same basic beliefs in God as creator, in Christ as the redeemer of the world, and in the Spirit as the one who makes Christ present in the church. In recent years, many attempts have been made to seek to overcome these differing perceptions of the church, with some degree of success. But in the meanwhile, over the last 200 years, another view of the church has developed, which cuts across these ancient divisions, and helps to place them in a new context.

## THIRD VIEW: THE CHURCH AS A VOCATIONAL COMMUNITY

For this view the church is no longer seen as the 'ark of salvation', in which alone humans can be saved from sin and find eternal life. It is rather seen as a community, alongside many others, which has a specific vocation or calling in the world. God offers salvation to all people, but very often they do not know what salvation is, or how they should find it. The Spirit will be at work in them in a hidden way, offering them choices for or against the love of God which they respond to, but do not recognise as such. The role of the church is to make known that hidden, universal work of the Spirit, so that people can recognise and respond consciously to it. The church will then mediate the presence and power of the Spirit in its truly adequate form – the form of self-giving, reconciling, serving love as it was expressed in Jesus.

The model at work here is Israel, the community of the first covenant. That community was not chosen for salvation, while all the rest of the world was left without the love of God. It was chosen to be loyal to the revelation of God given in Torah, and to become the 'priests of the earth' (Isaiah 61:6), proclaiming and making present that revelation of the divine mercy and loving-kindness, to all people. The church is the community of the new covenant, a people chosen by God to be devoted to God as he is revealed in the person of Jesus, and to make present that revelation as a real and transforming presence throughout the world.

The church thus has an important role in God's purpose for the world, but it exists as one religious community alongside others. Those other communities also often have distinctive insights into the divine nature, and the church must grow in understanding of its own disclosure by taking account of and living alongside these, in full respect for difference and diversity. The whole truth is not given in some original revelation, which must be preserved without change, and opposed to all other understandings of God and of the ultimate human purpose. Christians hold that God does truly disclose his nature and purpose in the events surrounding the life of Jesus. But the understanding of the implications of that disclosure, and of the divine purpose, needs to grow and develop in continuing interaction with other faith traditions and with growing scientific knowledge of the world. The church does guard a decisive moment of divine self-disclosure in Jesus, but it must also change and develop in a process of continually renewed understanding of the divine.

We do not know why some people are called to membership of the church, but we may be sure that it is not to be given eternal life, while everyone else perishes. It is to make the Spirit of universal and unconditional love known, through the proclamation of the life, death and resurrection of Jesus, through the sacraments which make the universal Christ who was manifested in Jesus present at many different times and places, and through serving the world in reconciling love, as Jesus did. If the church is the body of Christ, its role is to love, forgive, heal and seek out the lost and despairing, continuing the incarnation of the Christ in each present through the power of the Spirit.

The church should be one in love and fellowship, for everywhere it proclaims the same gospel, mediates the same reality of Christ, and serves others in his name. For this reason, it is desirable there should be some visible structure of unity, perhaps in union with a Supreme Pastor. But much more emphasis would be placed on the symbols, narratives and rites which express and mediate the divine reality as it was seen in Jesus, than on the theoretical formulation of propositional truths of faith. So the church would consist of a set of communities in which life-transforming experiences of God would be evoked and sustained, primarily by the use of symbols, narratives, metaphors and rituals. Propositional doctrines (the dogmas of faith) could be seen as theoretical reflections on these experiences and their metaphorical expressions, which would reflect the philosophies and world-views of particular ages and cultures, and would not of themselves be considered inerrant or irreformable.

The church could have real teaching authority, but that would consist in making available the best obtainable reflections on contemporary problems of faith and morality, with recommendations which would usually have great authority, without being formally binding on every individual conscience. The consequence would be that a variety of doctrinal and moral beliefs would be encouraged to exist, within the limits of a devotion to the nature and purposes of God disclosed in the life, death and resurrection of Jesus. Many past definitions might have to be revised or even rejected, as they show themselves to be incompatible with increasing knowledge of the world.

The renunciation of claims to inerrancy in Pope or Bible might seem too much for many traditional Christians. But in fact if claims to inerrancy were limited to the content of the apostolic witness to the life of Jesus, insofar as its truth was necessary for final salvation, there exists a possibility that agreement might be reached on these issues in future. In such a future united church, however, a great degree of pluralism – of variety of interpretation and belief – would have to be accepted, and freedom of conscientious dissent would have to be unreservedly protected.

On this view of the church, the sacraments remain vitally important, as they are the means by which the divine Spirit, in the form expressed in Jesus the Christ, is made present in many diverse communities. But the Mass, Eucharist or Lord's Supper would not be regarded as a sacrifice the primary purpose of which is to remove the sins of those who are present, or for whom it has been specifically offered. Just as the purpose of Jesus' self-offering was to make present the rule of God in human history, so the purpose of the offering of the Eucharist is to make present in a particular community the presence of the Spirit which will empower them to serve the world in love. Sharing in God's sacrifice of self for others, and in God's love which cannot be defeated by death, believers are empowered to live in the world as exemplars and mediators of that sacrificial love. So baptism is seen as a declaration of God's loving offer of salvation to us, made before we consciously respond, and as incorporation into the 'body of Christ', the community of those who try to make Christ present in the world in acts of forgiveness and reconciliation. There may be a ministry set apart to proclaim the gospel and celebrate the sacraments, but it will be considered important to affirm the full equality of all human beings before God by ordaining both men and women to that ministry.

No doubt such a calling will prove very hard to follow, and the church will actually remain very largely the sort of ambiguous and sinful community that all human communities are. Nevertheless, what is called for is a rejection of the image of the church as a safe haven, cut off from the world, into which the 'elect' might retreat. That image must be replaced by the image of the church as a community of creative, contemplative and compassionate love, whose calling is to transform the whole material world into an expression and vehicle of the divine Spirit. It is in that active and redemptive sense that the church is called to be the body of Christ, the continuing means by which God enters into time to unite it to the life of eternity.

This third view of the church does not form a new tradition, like Catholicism or Protestantism. It could exist within both Catholic and Protestant churches, and to some extent it already does so. These forms of understanding of the nature of the Christian community will probably continue to co-exist, but they may each be modified as they interact with one another, and Christians continue to seek for the most appropriate form of the body of Christ in a changing world.

# 11 THE BIBLE

Different Christian churches are distinguished from one another largely by their differing attitudes to authority and the way it is exercised. All Christians, however, accept that the ultimate authority for faith is the person of Jesus, in and through whom God revealed the nature of divine love and the way to salvation. It is therefore important for Christianity that there should be some trustworthy testimony to Jesus' life and teachings, which can be passed on to future generations. All Christians also accept that the basic source of this testimony is the Bible, which provides the foundation for subsequent Christian prayer and reflection. Because of its importance for preserving the apostolic witness to the person of Jesus, the Bible has come to be seen as itself a book inspired by God, though there are various ways of interpreting the nature of this inspiration.

The Bible is in fact a whole library of books (the word 'Bible' comes from a Greek word meaning 'the books'). These books are of many different kinds. There are stories, histories, poems, letters, proverbs and prophecies. They were written and edited over a long period of time. In its present form the Bible is a selection from a much wider set of documents, which had taken its present form by the second century CE, and was more or less agreed by the fourth century CE. There are slight differences between the Roman Catholic and other Christian churches as to which books are included in the Bible (the disputed books form the 'Apocrypha', or 'Hidden things', coming after most Old Testament books, which Roman Catholics accept as fully inspired, but others regard as having a secondary status). But the 66 main books of the Old and New Testament are printed in all Bibles.

For a Christian, the most important part of the Bible is the New Testament, which consists of four 'gospels' – accounts of the life and teachings of Jesus – and a number of letters from the early years of the church, together with the mysterious symbolism of the 'Revelation of John'. The four gospels are very different from one another. They are written for different groups of readers, and they each have a special slant which the editor of each one has given them. The letters, too, are from different writers and to different groups of believers, and they express rather different viewpoints on what Christian faith is.

The thing that holds the whole collection together, however, is that they all focus on Jesus as the Messiah, the one who frees human beings from the power of sin and opens up the way to eternal life to all who follow him. The Bible is the only written source for knowledge of Jesus, and for the beliefs of many of his earliest followers. Attempts to 'go behind' the gospels to discover what the real historical Jesus was like can never be more than speculative guesses, which will largely depend on what historians think of the genuineness and probable truth of the gospels. What we incontestably possess is good evidence for what many groups of early Christians thought about Jesus, his life and teaching, and about the impact of faith on their lives. All Christians would accept so much, though the exact place they then give to the authority of the Bible differs.

## FIRST VIEW: THE BIBLE AS INERRANT NORM OF FAITH

Because the Bible is the only source of information about Jesus, on whom Christianity is founded, many Christians believe that it must be protected from error by God, so that the revelation of God in

Jesus will not be corrupted or distorted. The Old Testament prophesies the coming of the Messiah, and so it is necessary to understand the role of Jesus in the story of salvation. The New Testament lays down the basic outlines of what is to be believed and done in the name of Christ. Traditional Christians of all denominations hold that Scripture is inspired by the Spirit of God. Even though it is written by many different authors, and collected together by many different groups of people, the Spirit ensures that it expresses the very thoughts of God, which remain definitive for Christianity. At the Reformation, Protestants like John Calvin (1509–64) argued that the Bible should be the sole norm of faith, so that any church teachings which contradict Biblical doctrines must be rejected, and any teachings not found in the Bible must be regarded as optional. Roman Catholics insisted that tradition should be accepted in addition to the Bible. Exactly what 'tradition' consists in has never been closely defined. It would, however, include the decisions of church councils, formulating such things as the doctrine of the Trinity or of the Assumption of Mary, which are not explicitly stated in the Bible. And it would include the authority of the church to interpret the Bible by the guidance of the Holy Spirit.

The Roman Catholic view allows for a greater degree of freedom of interpretation and development of doctrine, although that freedom will be fully possessed only by the magisterium (the official teaching body) of the church. Since many things are not explicit in the Bible, Protestants are free to develop many views in disputed or novel areas, none of which will possess the authority of revelation. As a matter of fact, most of the key Christian beliefs – about the nature of the incarnation and of the Trinity, about salvation and about the nature of God – are not systematically developed in Scripture at all. So it is not surprising that Protestants who insist on the inerrancy of Scripture tend to split into hundreds of sects, differing about exactly what Scripture says. The obvious conclusion is that Scripture, while indisputably teaching that Jesus is the Messiah and Saviour of the world, does not have one specific and definitive view on most of these matters. It is hard for some Christians to accept that many different opinions are possible on such central matters of faith, but ironically those who insist on the sole sufficiency of Scripture for salvation are committed to exactly such a pluralism of interpretations.

In one sense, then, insistence on the inerrancy of Scripture does not help to resolve major problems of truth in Christian belief. This in turn tends to undermine the argument that God must have provided one clear and specific revelation – for Biblical revelation is very unclear and unspecific in so many ways. One should not exaggerate the unclarity and vagueness of Scripture, however, since there is no doubt that it declares that the love of God is manifested in Jesus, that he died to save humanity, and that he rose again to give eternal life to those who follow him.

For many Christians, however, this is not enough. Believing that the Bible is spoken by God, they will admit no error in it. All historical events must have happened as reported. All the teachings of Jesus and of the letter-writers of the New Testament must be followed as divine law. The Biblical texts contain the words of God, and to criticise them is to criticise God himself.

## SECOND VIEW: THE BIBLE AS WITNESS TO REVELATION

A great many Christians, even in very traditional churches, would not insist on such strict and total inerrancy, even of the Biblical texts. Most Christians today think that the creation accounts in Genesis, for example, are poetic or mythical, not scientifically accurate. The accounts may be mistaken about the details of the origin of the physical universe, but they convey a spiritual message in symbolic terms which is importantly true. The same might be said of prophecies about the end of the world or the highly symbolic language in which the New Testament sometimes speaks of the return of Christ in glory. Again, it is widely held that the four Gospels should not be read as purely factual accounts, all of whose details are correct. They are primarily texts for Christian worship, and many of the details are presented as symbols of spiritual truths, or perhaps as incidental material whose exact accuracy is unimportant to the sense of the text as a whole. So one may speak in a rather guarded way, and say that the Scripture is infallible with regard to everything that God wills to teach as necessary to salvation – leaving it vague as to what exactly this covers. This is the present attitude of the Roman Catholic church, as stated at the second Vatican Council (*Dei Verbum*, 1965), and it is probably the view of the major Protestant churches.

One theological reason for taking such a more guarded view is that, unlike the Qur'an, the Bible does not claim to be dictated by God word for word. Very few Christians have taken a 'dictation' view of the inspiration of the Holy Spirit. It is more typical to think of the Spirit as overseeing the writings of many different individuals, to ensure that, taken together, they convey insight into spiritual truth, without putting words one by one into their minds. The different books of the Bible are written in very different styles. Some of them are extremely pessimistic (Ecclesiastes, for example) and some almost naively optimistic (some of the Psalms). It seems clear that the personalities and beliefs of the writers were not simply over-ridden by the Spirit, but rather used to build up a set of documents which would, as a whole, give insight into the nature and purposes of God.

If the centre of Christian revelation is the person of Jesus, it is not perhaps without significance that Jesus never wrote a book or dictated teachings to his disciples, to be committed to memory (as Muhammad, for instance, did). He taught in obscure parables and incredible aphorisms, but not in a systematic or detailed way. This suggests that Christian faith is not primarily a set of doctrines, and that revelation is not in a set of propositions, to be memorised and handed on to future generations intact. Christian faith is, as the Gospels perhaps suggest, a disclosure of the personal reality of God in and through the person of Jesus. Christian revelation is the making-present of that personal reality in new and vital ways to many generations of men and women, so that they can receive and interpret it in terms of their own cultural and temperamental presuppositions.

What the Gospels do is to witness to the person of Jesus as the one who makes God present and active. It is in that way, perhaps, that he makes the kingdom of God (which equals the rule of God in human lives) present to those who encounter him. For this to be so, the Bible needs to be a trustworthy witness to the events in which God discloses himself. But it does not have to be inerrant in every detail.

One could say, for example, that the death of Jesus and his appearing to the disciples after his death must be actual occurrences, if Christianity is true at all. But which of the disciples got to the tomb first, or exactly what time it was, are things about which one might expect a little vagueness of memory on the part of those who recounted them to the Gospel writers. Such details are not important to the central truths of faith. The Bible is not dictated inerrantly by God, but it is inspired by God, and it witnesses to the acts of God in and through the life of Jesus, and especially in his death and resurrection. Such events might not have been fully understood, but they form the unchangeable core upon which all subsequent Christian reflection is based. The Christian revelation, on this view, is not wholly inerrant or exclusively true. But it is normative, in that it gives an unrevisably correct disclosure of God as suffering, redeeming love, discerned in the person of Jesus, and imaginatively expressed in the Scriptures.

## THIRD VIEW: THE BIBLE AS RECORD OF REVELATORY EXPERIENCE

Some Christians would go a great deal further than this, and say that there is no reason to expect infallibility of the Bible, any more than of any other religious text. There may be errors of fact – about whether demons really exist, and can be exorcised, for example – and even failures of moral perception – as when women are told to be obedient to men. The beliefs of the Biblical writers remained limited by the culture of their day. Those who hold such a view may hold that accounts of the character, teachings and acts of Jesus recorded in the Gospels are accurate overall, though they contain elements of myth and legend as well. More radical Christians may think that most of the Gospel accounts are legendary, the product of later reflection on experiences within the early Christian community. For them, the core of faith is likely to be the experience of new life and freedom in the early church, which was evoked by the death of Jesus and by the belief that he had been raised from death by God. The story of the historical Jesus becomes a myth or symbol for evoking and sustaining that sort of experience, which is to be repeated in the life of believers in each new generation. The Christian experience may then be seen as one form of religious experience, which is distinctive in being founded in some way, however indirect, on the life of Jesus, as apprehended by faith. The Bible is the definitive record of this distinctive sort of experience, generated by encounter with Jesus, which originated in the early Christian churches. This view is mostly associated with what is sometimes called liberal Protestantism, originating largely with the work of the Prussian theologian Friedrich Schleiermacher (1768–1834).

These three understandings of Biblical revelation may seem very different. Yet there are deep agreements present, which enable them to co-exist as explorations of Christian faith. Whether the historical records of the life of Jesus in the four Gospels are wholly inerrant, or are generally accurate expressions of the acts of God in and through Jesus, or are mythical expressions of a new sort of living experience of God, all Christians accept that the Gospels present Jesus as the fount and origin of a new understanding of divine love, of a way of sharing in the divine love, and of a hope for the ultimate triumph of divine love, that is capable of illuminating the world. The Bible is the normative testimony to that perception of faith, and for that reason alone it will always be the central resource and inspiration of the Christian faith.

# 12 THE TEACHING OF JESUS

The Bible presents Jesus as the originator of a new understanding of God and a new way of relating to God. So it is important to understand something of the teaching of Jesus. In a short introduction like this, there is no possibility of exploring that teaching fully, but I will try to pick out what I believe to be some main features of his teaching, as it is presented in the Gospels, focusing particularly on the so-called 'sermon on the mount' (Matthew 5–7). This is a collection of sayings on a number of related themes, edited into one continuous sermon by the gospel writer, and forming the longest continuous piece of teaching material in the first three ('synoptic') gospels.

One thing that is fairly certain about Jesus is that he taught the kingdom of God was at hand. It is not so certain, however, what he meant by this. Did he think of the kingdom of God as a renewal of the Davidic monarchy in Israel, and was he saying that this would happen very soon, throwing the occupying Roman forces out of the land of Israel? Or did he think of the kingdom as some sort of cataclysmic supernatural event, which would bring the present form of history to an end, and usher in the Day of Judgement? Or again, was he speaking in a largely metaphorical way about the rule of God in the hearts of men and women, and was he saying that in his own person the rule of God drew near to them? Did he look for the birth of a new, more inward and spiritual form of divine–human covenant, when the law would be written on people's hearts, not on tablets of stone (Jeremiah 31:33), and when there would be a new community in human history (the church), indwelt by the Spirit of God?

It may seem strange that there is so much uncertainty about such a central item of Jesus' teaching. But in fact a similar uncertainty extends to almost everything the Gospels record him as saying. Did he, for example, keep the Jewish Law, the Torah, or did he teach people that it was not important? The evidence seems to point both ways. Mark's gospel records that he 'declared all foods clean' (Mark 7:19), which implies that he was prepared to put aside the kosher food laws. But Matthew's gospel, while insisting that he had the authority to interpret the Law in new ways, records that he insisted that the least jot and tittle of the Law should be kept by his hearers (Matthew 5:18). You can argue the case both ways. The point is that we do not really know what Jesus thought about keeping Torah.

Even on the topic of divorce, one of the few specific ethical issues he addresses, the matter is unclear. Did he permit divorce and remarriage, or did he prohibit it? Matthew and Paul both consider that there are circumstances when divorce (and therefore remarriage, in the Jewish context) is permissible (namely, when adultery or sexual infidelity has taken place, or when one partner is not a Christian; Matthew 5, 32:1; Corinthians 7:15). But Mark seems to prohibit it completely (Mark 10, 11, 12). It is not surprising that different churches take different interpretations. On the whole, Roman Catholics think that he prohibited divorce, and so they do likewise (though they have a procedure for ruling that many apparent marriages have not in fact taken place, and are annulled). Most Protestants and the Eastern Orthodox think that he allowed divorce, and therefore remarriage, in certain circumstances, and they do the same.

Whatever our own views may be, therefore, we have to admit that, on the evidence of the Bible alone, it is just not clear exactly what Jesus taught about how his followers should live. Of course it would be silly to say that we have no idea at all of what Jesus taught. At the very least, we know from the Gospels what many early Christians thought he had taught. Those accounts present Jesus' teachings from different perspectives and with different slants, but some things seem clear.

Though Jesus taught in parables, designed to make his teachings obscure (Mark 4: 11–12), it is fairly clear that the 'Kingdom' is a state which one can enter or exclude oneself from. To enter the Kingdom requires renunciation of pride, renunciation of the love of money, the cultivation of innocence of mind, and compassion for friends and enemies alike. One must put God's rule even above love of family, and to accept it means turning away from all anxious concern with possessions. To keep the letter of Torah is not enough. It is the heart which must be changed and renewed, so that love for God and for God's creation always takes precedence over selfish desires or commitment to a specific family or ethnic group.

There can be no doubt that Jesus was believed to have called for a total and radical devotion to God, a God who commanded love for all. Perhaps the heart of his teaching is that if one makes such a commitment, it is then part of Christian discipleship to work out particular moral issues for oneself. If that is true, it will not seem so strange that Jesus did not issue lists of rules or commandments, which his disciples were to memorise or write down. The Jewish Torah contains (by tradition) 613 different commands. They cover very detailed matters like what things to eat, what not to do on the Sabbath, and how to conduct sacrifices. According to the Gospels, Jesus did recommend keeping at least the main commandments, and he described the two most important commandments as loving God and loving one's neighbour (Matthew 22:37–40). He apparently differed with the religious authorities in his interpretation of many of the commandments, putting human need above keeping the rules regardless of context. In the sermon on the mount, he takes a number of commandments or traditions, and provides a very radical interpretation of them, penetrating to their inner meaning.

But did he mean these interpretations to be followed as literal rules? Though Christians will often say that they should live by the teaching of the sermon on the mount, in fact Christians have different views about just how to take Jesus' teaching in this respect.

## FIRST VIEW: HEROIC MORAL RULES

What happens if we try to take the sermon on the mount as literally as possible? Anger and contempt of others is prohibited (except anger for just cause, according to some manuscripts). Regarding another as an object of sexual desire is prohibited (unless one is married, presumably). Divorce is prohibited. Swearing on oath is prohibited. Revenge and hatred of enemies is prohibited. Praying and fasting ostentatiously in public is prohibited. Concern about food and clothes is prohibited. Judging others is prohibited. More positively, one must seek reconciliation with those one might have offended. One must be absolutely faithful and truthful. One must not resist an evil person, but must 'turn the other cheek', give to anyone who asks anything of one, and always 'walk the extra mile'. One must love enemies, and do good to all.

Few can read this sermon and fail to feel admiration for the ideal of human life expressed in it. It is harder, however, to see just how to apply it in one's own life. How should we put into practice, for instance, the command that we should give to anyone who asks, and that we should not resist an evil person? On one interpretation of these commands, we should very soon have no money left at all, and we should in all probability be quickly enslaved, abused or killed by ruthless dictators and military oppressors.

There have always been those who have nevertheless insisted that the commands should be followed as closely as possible. If that means that we will be penniless, mocked and enslaved, we are then following in the way of the Cross, following the master who had no house, no possessions, and who was mocked and killed. Christians are called to be a 'little flock', and perhaps they will be despised and abused by the world. On the other hand, perhaps they will, like leaven in dough, slowly affect the character of the world itself, and by their witness to self-giving love, they may transform and perhaps finally overcome the violence and conflict of human nature.

So, throughout Christian history, there have been heroic groups of disciples committed to pacifism and poverty, ready to be 'fools for Christ' in a world of war, hatred and possessive greed. They refuse to accept that their deaths are defeats, for God will not be mocked, and trust in God's providence requires following his commands in the faith that he will bring all things to good in his own way. Certainly, pragmatic considerations can never over-rule the divine command of unconditional love, which makes all thoughts of violence, greed, hatred and lust impossible.

That way, however, is not open to all of us. The problem is familiar. We will do more good by accumulating as much money as we lawfully can, then using it responsibly and carefully, than by giving it away to anyone who asks. We will save more lives by resisting murderers and rapists, by imprisoning them, judging them and punishing them, than by loving them indiscriminately and refusing to curtail their activities. If we think this, we will not be able to embrace a life of poverty and pacifism. We will be committed to the responsible accumulation and use of wealth, and to some use of force to restrain evil. If we are to be involved in the political rule of a state, it will even be our obligation to deploy both wealth and force responsibly. What then can we do with the sermon on the mount?

## SECOND VIEW: COUNSELS OF PERFECTION

One possibility, which has been quite widely adopted, is to distinguish between precepts of morality, which everyone is absolutely obliged to keep, and counsels of perfection, which are binding only on those called to the higher way of Christian perfection. Examples of precepts would be the command not to take innocent human life, or not to steal for personal gain. These may be absolute moral commands, which there is no justification for breaking, and which everyone is able to keep if they try. Examples of counsels of perfection would be the command not to have any personal property, or the command never to use force against others for any reason.

On this interpretation, some people are called to the way of perfection – monks and nuns are, perhaps, but also small groups of lay Christians. Most Christians, however, will not be bound by the counsels of perfection, though they should honour their pursuit by others. This interpretation is characteristic of the Catholic tradition. Protestant Christians tend to be suspicious of it, because it seems to create a sort of hierarchy of spiritual perfection, with some Christians being at a higher level than others. Protestants generally do not have monasteries and convents, since they think that Christians should be fully in the world, and not enclosed in what may seem to be privileged isolation. So they are unhappy with a way of interpreting the sermon which may seem to give monks and nuns a higher status than ordinary Christians, who have to struggle with the complexities of family and political responsibility. Most Protestants want to qualify the extremely demanding rules of the sermon in some way, but not by limiting them to a fairly arbitrary class of people.

One influential Protestant way of interpreting the sermon is that of Martin Luther, who insisted that Jesus' sayings should be taken in their full rigour, and applied to everyone without exception. The twist in Luther's argument is that he admitted that a literal following of the sermon is impossible. What the sermon places before us is precisely an 'impossible possibility'. We ought to do what it says, but we cannot. This, of course, contradicts directly what many feel to be an axiom of morality – that we must be able to do what we ought to do. But Luther thought that, because we are estranged from God, there is something radically wrong with the human will. We have duties we can never obey. We are condemned to be sinners in the eyes of God. We are, to put it differently, morally incapable because of the corruption of human nature.

It may seem that the acceptance of such a total moral incapacity should lead to neurosis and depression. But in Luther's view it actually should lead to a tremendous sense of release. After all, human incapacity is not the end of the story, since God freely forgives our sin and restores us to relationship with him. When we realise that we are incapable, we should feel released from the tyranny of constant moral endeavour, from the constant questioning of whether we have made enough moral effort, and from the danger of self-righteousness when we do happen to do something right. None of our moral efforts will ever be enough, so we are let off the hook. We can relax, because God will do in us what we cannot do for ourselves. His forgiveness is free, and his sanctification is total.

Luther in this way recaptures some of Paul's sense that he was released from the constant striving to obey all the injunctions of Torah. Once he realised that he could never do so, that obedience to law would never 'justify' him before God, he was free, he felt, to surrender himself wholly and simply to God's free forgiving love. So Paul teaches that acceptance with God is not a matter of 'works', of moral effort, but of 'free grace', of God's forgiveness (see Paul's letter to the Romans, chapters 2–8). On this view, the sermon has the primary purpose of making quite clear to us our moral incapacity, and therefore our need for the forgiveness of God. Morality remains in full force, but its demands are much more strenuous than we might ever have imagined. And in the end, it is not our moral success that matters, but simply our acceptance of God's forgiving grace.

Of course, this view has the danger, as Paul saw, of making people feel that morality is not important after all. If we are saved by grace, why should we not sin without guilt? The answer to that puzzle is very simple. If we are truly saved by grace, then God's power will work in us to produce the fruits of the Spirit, of love, peace, patience, joy and goodness. This will not be the result of our desperate efforts, but of the effortless power of God's love flooding into our hearts, as we turn to him. Morality of itself can only condemn; but God's grace both frees us from that condemnation and empowers us to love in freedom.

## THIRD VIEW: IDEALS OF THE HEART

For those who are unable to accept that there can be impossible moral demands, or rules limited to just one group of specially 'religious' people, another type of interpretation is available. Perhaps Jesus' comments are examples of hyperbole, of exaggerated statement intended to make a point in an exceptionally memorable way, not to give a rule to be followed literally.

There is no doubt that Jesus often used hyperbole. When he said it was harder for a camel to get through a needle's eye than for a rich man to enter the kingdom (Matthew 19:24), and when he said that we should cut off our hands and pull out our eyes if they offend us (Matthew 5:29, 30), these were exaggerated statements. We remember them precisely because they are exaggerated. But if we ask exactly what they mean, it is impossible to turn them into precise principles. He did not mean that no rich people could get to heaven. Abraham is there, for a start, and Jesus adds that with God all things are possible. He did not mean that churches should have surgeons standing ready to cut off the hands of penitents. Presumably he meant that riches are dangerous to a spiritual outlook, and that we should be very careful what we look at and do. But there is no rule which says just how much money we are allowed to have, or what exactly is offensive about eyes. So the sermon could consist of a set of hyperboles, not of precise moral rules.

Does that mean that the sermon's injunctions to give to all who ask, and to turn the other cheek, are irrelevant to most Christians? Most Christians would not say these injunctions are irrelevant, but perhaps they would agree that they are not to be taken as unbreakable and strictly binding rules. They might rather be taken as ideals of personal life, not as rules of social life.

A rule of social life is a rule everyone must follow, and everyone has a right to expect everyone else to follow. Anyone who breaks such a rule deserves to be punished. An ideal of personal life is something that individuals may take as an ideal they would like to follow, and try to follow as far as possible, but need not always follow. No one has a right to expect others to live up to such ideals, and anyone who fails to do so does not deserve to be punished.

As an example, I may have as a personal ideal the principle that I should be absolutely truthful. That means that I should never knowingly tell a lie. But it also means that I should never conceal the truth, that I should be completely open in my thoughts and actions, so that there is no deceit and no concealment of my motives and intentions at any time. When you think about it, you soon realise that the ideal of absolute truthfulness is extremely difficult to put into practice. Suppose I am on the appointing committee for a very important job, and that I know what all my fellow committee members think about the various applicants. One of those applicants asks me what a certain committee member thinks of her. Of course I could refuse to answer, and almost certainly I should do so. But this is being less than absolutely open and truthful. It is knowingly concealing something I know to be true, because I think the knowledge would be harmful, or because I have promised not to reveal it. So absolute truthfulness is probably impossible in most human societies.

I can still have absolute truthfulness as an ideal, however. I can try to be absolutely open with others, as much as I possibly can. I can be thinking of ways in which I can be more open, and be trying to think of ways to make absolute truthfulness more characteristic of my society. But there will be many times when I cannot live up to that ideal, and when it would not even be right to do so. Yet others are in no position to blame me for that. As long as I keep the precept of not actually lying, I have done my duty. Many Christians will feel, however, that it is not enough just to do one's basic duties. One must also strive as much as possible to live up to one's personal ideals, though we can never really tell if we have done all that we can.

Absolute truthfulness is one of the principles of the sermon on the mount. What this interpretation is suggesting is in effect that we should split this principle into two parts. First of all, there is the precept of not lying for personal gain, which is binding on everyone.

Second, there is the counsel of being absolutely honest at all times. Most Christians will not be able to live up to that, and perhaps sometimes should not do so, but they should always try to do as much as they can reasonably do to be absolutely honest.

An even better example is the counsel to love our neighbours as ourselves. Given that Jesus says that everyone is our neighbour (Luke 10:29–37), this is telling us that we should never prefer our own good over that of others. As a strict duty, this seems hopeless. I could never go to the theatre without first offering my ticket to someone else, and I could never have a good meal while anyone in the world was starving.

The strict duty here – what we actually demand that everyone does – is that one should never knowingly harm innocent people, and that one should be charitable to a reasonable degree. But loving others as ourselves is an ideal. It is a reminder that we should consider the needs of others and work for their welfare. It does not tell us how much we have to do, or when it is reasonable to have a day off and enjoy ourselves.

The ideal of universal love places before us a standard of perfection which we can never live up to, but it always spurs us on a little further than we actually reach. It reminds us that we are 'in sin' and that we live in a sinful world. That is, we are not filled with the divine love, which alone could enable us to give up our lives and at the same time to fulfil them, by receiving God's love and naturally communicating it to others. Only divine wisdom could tell us how to do that, and only divine power could enable us to do it. It is because we are cut off from divine wisdom and power that we do not know how much to love, or in what way to love, and that we are not able naturally and effortlessly and joyfully to love. The truth is that we cannot love others fully if we are not first filled with an overwhelming power of love ourselves. Such love can only come from God, and it is because we lack a deep relationship with God that love can be for us only an impossible, but constantly challenging, ideal.

On this interpretation, the sermon on the mount takes us beyond morality to relationship with God. It reveals the depth of our estrangement from God, and so our need of forgiveness. It reveals the inadequacy of moral effort to heal the alienation of human life from its own fundamental reality. It reveals the nature of the divine love, which alone is truly self-giving, universal and unconditional. And so it reveals that the Christian life is not one of increasing moral success. It is one of continuing repentance (knowledge of our human inadequacy) and dependence upon the power of God, upon grace alone. Penitence without grace might be a mournful and sorrowful thing. But Christian penitence rests on the assured knowledge of divine forgiveness and love, and for that reason it is a spontaneous and joyful thing.

If one applies this sort of analysis to the injunctions to give to those who ask, and to turn the other cheek, they will be interpreted as telling us to give liberally (but not saying how much, to whom, or when), and to renounce the desire for revenge (but not prohibiting any use of force for the sake of justice).

Those who take this interpretation will argue that Jesus could not have been actually revoking Torah, with its provision of retribution (an eye for an eye) and its view that the wealth of the Patriarchs was a sign of blessing from God. This is particularly so, because the sermon begins with an affirmation of the importance of even the smallest of the commandments of Torah.

What Jesus was doing, then, was showing how the commands of Torah have a sort of double level. They state duties of social life, which can be kept by anyone if they try. But there is an inner level, where they speak to us of ideals of the heart, ideals of total respect for others, fidelity, open-ness, benevolence and non-possessiveness. At this level, Jesus shows us what human life should be and what divine life is. He brings that divine life close to us, offers forgiveness for our incapacity and a way of sharing in the love of God which will fit us eventually for membership of a community – the kingdom of God – in which those ideals can be fully implemented, because it lives wholly by the power of the love of God.

What, on this interpretation, did Jesus mean by saying, 'Repent, for the kingdom of God is at hand'? If he was speaking of a community which lives wholly by the power of God, then that kingdom will remain future and unrealised until the whole history of human freedom and human sin has come to an end. Its realisation will be beyond this space and time, and in a realm beyond corruption, suffering and sin. Yet Jesus did not say, 'The kingdom of God is millions of years in the future, or even nowhere in this universe'. He said, 'It is at hand'. The rule of God, to be completed only beyond history, comes close to men and women as they hear the words of Jesus, feel the presence of Jesus, and by repentance turn to rely as wholly upon God as they can. The kingdom begins now, in the hearts of men and women who receive the power of God's love, but it will be completed beyond historical time, when the whole creation is renewed by God's power.

These interpretations of the sermon are different, but they all agree that Jesus' teaching was both striking and profound, that it challenged people's ordinary moral assumptions, and led them to connect moral action with the love of God. Christians should seek to live under the rule of the spirit of love, and that spirit is the power of God which is given to them, a spirit patterned on the life and teaching of Jesus. He is the exemplar of the spirit-filled life, and to live the Christian life is not so much to have special moral rules. It is rather to be filled with the spirit of self-giving and joyful love.

# 13 CHRISTIANITY AND ETHICS

Christianity is not primarily about providing special moral rules. Nevertheless it is concerned with morality, and it is not possible to divorce Christianity from the attempt to live a good human life, and to make such a life possible for others. Christians, like most theists, believe that God has a purpose for the human world, and so living rightly will consist in helping to realise that purpose. If the purpose is the creation of communities of love and justice, then realising God's purpose will at the same time be a striving to realise love and justice in human communities. For Christians, morality and the worship of God cannot be separated. Devotion to God is not some private spiritual activity, which has no relation to the principles of political and moral life in society. Devotion to God entails obedience to God. That entails seeking to realise God's purpose. And that means striving for justice and love in human societies.

In the Old Testament, the Torah lays down principles for living together in society. Those principles are meant to set Israel apart as a special community devoted to God, and also to be an example of justice and mercy to the whole world. The food laws and laws of ritual purity remind the observant Jew that all of life is under the direction of God, who wills life, health and integrity of mind and body. The sacrificial and festival laws outline the right way of relating to God – a way of reverence, thanksgiving and joy, when the good things one possesses are to be shared with the poor and resident aliens. Laws concerning the remission of debts and liberation of slaves are reminders that our goods are only borrowed from God, and are to be used in the service of others. Laws concerned with justice and punishment for crime inculcate respect for human life, and emphasise the importance of honesty, fairness and promise-keeping. Laws concerning kindness and mercy are reminders that all life is given by God, and must be cherished as his gift.

So the Torah is not a legalistic and oppressive set of regulations. It is an outline of the proper response to a God who liberates from slavery and wills life and happiness for all his creatures. Jesus was brought up in the observance of Torah, and there is little doubt that his family would have been observant Jews. Most of the apostles observed Torah, and Peter was reluctant to preach to or even eat with Gentiles at first. Yet the fact is that the Christian church gave up the practice of Torah within the first generation. From that time on, Christians have not had a body of divinely revealed law which governs their daily lives. Nevertheless, many Christians seek to make their moral decisions compatible with Biblical teaching, and so far as possible to derive their moral principles from the Bible. Because the written law has been given up, this requires great sensitivity and discrimination. The Bible does need interpreting, but many Christians feel that, if used rightly, it is in a way self-interpreting.

## FIRST VIEW: THE BIBLE AS THE BASIS OF ETHICS

Naturally enough, Christians take the New Testament as the clue to interpreting the rest of the Bible. All the commands of the Old Testament need to be interpreted in the light of the fact that the sacrificial system was taken to be completed in Jesus, and the food and ritual laws, which were meant to set apart the Jews as a special people, were superseded by the fact that Gentiles were accepted into the Church. So the 613 commandments of the Old Testament were radically transformed by the fact that the new, largely Gentile, community of the church took its source of moral guidance, not from a set of written laws, but from the life of Jesus. It is not that the Torah becomes unimportant, but that it is fulfilled in a personal life, which becomes the chief moral inspiration for Christians. The commandments remain as guides to ethical reflection, but they are summed up, for Christians, in the one principle of loving God with all one's heart, and loving others as oneself (Romans 13:8–10).

Calvin took the view that all the ritual and food laws of Torah had been fulfilled in Jesus, so were no longer binding. But the moral laws, like the Ten Commandments (Exodus 20:1–17), remain an important moral guideline. In general, these commandments are, he held, to be interpreted in a very rigorous sense. Thus it is not only that one ought not to kill unlawfully, but one should positively seek to preserve human life. One should not only refrain from stealing. One should positively share one's goods with others. And so on.

Many traditional Protestants do regard many of the injunctions in the New Testament as commands, which should never be changed or disobeyed. The most important commandment of all, after the command to obey God, is that one should respect human life. Since humans are created in the image of God, to destroy a human life is to destroy God's image. Moreover, every human life is a life for which Jesus sacrificed himself, and so it becomes of very great worth (some might say of infinite worth). Humans are meant to have eternal life, and since that may well depend on what they do in this life, it becomes of ultimate importance to give them every opportunity for turning to God, and not to take away the lives God has given.

There is no direct Biblical teaching on such difficult problems as abortion and euthanasia, but most traditional Christians would hold that it is always wrong directly to take human life. There may be very difficult cases, however, in which the life of a mother may be at stake if an embryo is not aborted, or in which someone is dying in extreme pain. In such cases, it may be held that the life of the mother can be preserved by abortion, and that an agonising death can be hastened. But these problems are widely disputed, and are not solved by the

Bible itself. What is clear is that nothing must be done which undermines respect for human life as given by God. It is no accident that Christians have been responsible for founding hospitals, hospices and homes for the destitute wherever they have been able to do so. And the abolition of slavery was largely sponsored by evangelical Christians who saw that slavery was incompatible with true respect for others.

The Christian stress on the sanctity of human life is a tremendously important moral insight. In modern times, we are more aware that animal life, too, is worthy of respect, and cannot be treated with indifference or cruelty. The Bible does not say much about animals, but humans are clearly given a responsibility to care for the earth (Genesis 1:28), and so it would seem natural to care for animals, since they, like humans, have life 'breathed into' them by God. This has been a neglected area in Christian moral thought, but the requirement of universal love must, one would think, apply to animals as well as to human beings, even though humans are objects of special respect, because of their possession of rational and moral responsibility.

Difficult moral issues are raised by the belief of some New Testament writers that women must obey their husbands (Ephesians 5:22), that divorce and sex outside monogamous marriage is not permissible (1 Corinthians 7:10, 11), and that homosexual practice is sinful (1 Corinthians 6:9, 10). There is no doubt that these views are present in the New Testament. The question is whether they represent culturally specific beliefs that do not apply in all contexts, or whether they are meant to lay down absolute moral rules for all time.

There will always be Biblical Christians who take them to be absolute rules. But there are reasons for doubting whether this is a fully Biblical view. One reason is that the subordination of women seems a very similar case to the subordination of certain people as slaves. The New Testament never condemns slavery, but it came to be seen as incompatible with universal respect for human life. In accordance with such a principle of universal respect, women should be respected equally with men, and this is not consistent with requiring them to obey men, however stupid the men are and however wise the women are. So we might well say these comments are due to a certain failure of the New Testament writers to see just what was implied in Jesus' command for universal love and respect. They failed to see the inadequacy of slavery, just as they also failed to see the problems in the rule that everyone should obey the state authorities, however bad those authorities are.

Of course, this sort of interpretation would mean that the New Testament writers were still working out the implications of Jesus' life and teaching for morality, and had not yet seen all of them. One might argue that is a very Biblical view to take, since Paul, in the letter to the Romans, constantly repeats that Christ has brought the law to an end, and we are to live henceforth not by the written letter of the law, but in the Spirit (Romans 10:4). Perhaps the Christian moral life has to be worked out over many years, and we have not seen all its implications even yet. All rules, even the New Testament ones, are provisional – as the Old Testament rules obviously are for Christians.

The New Testament teachings on divorce and homosexuality seem to be similar. When one remembers that polygamy was normal in the Old Testament, that marriages were arranged, and that concubinage was accepted without criticism, it becomes clear that the idea of monogamous marriage in its modern form is not actually enjoined in the Bible. Here again, just as there was development from the Old to the New Testaments, so there may be further developments in the life of the church. Those developments, however, must always proceed in the direction of love and respect for human lives, and never become an excuse for selfish greed or desire. Perhaps, in the end, that is the final test.

With regard to social ethics, the situation is again not wholly clear. Some passages seem to recommend distancing oneself from the political process altogether, renouncing the world and embracing lives of poverty and total non-violence (James 4:4). Yet in the Old Testament the Patriarchs were blessed by God with wealth, and were commanded to take Canaan by force. Moses established a judiciary at the command of God, and set out a code of laws to enable society to function in a just and merciful way. Moreover, the conditions of political life have changed considerably since New Testament times, when Christians were a small largely disadvantaged group within a militaristic foreign Empire. When they became the established church of that Empire, their leaders part of the ruling elite, New Testament principles were put in a very different context.

It is not surprising, then, that Biblical views of political thought can include those who advocate a complete separation from the political process (which is seen to belong to 'the world' and its structures, which are doomed to perdition). They also include a radical prophetic strain of opposition to perceived injustices and established privilege in society (modelled on the prophets, who opposed Kings in the name of the poor). And they include a conservative concern to perpetuate social systems which preserve the values of family, private property and institutions for the promotion of virtue and the punishment of vice. All these views can find some basis in the Bible, and decisions about which to accept will partly depend upon whether one sees Jesus as someone who allowed himself to be killed by the powers of this world, or as a prophetic revolutionary in the name of justice, or as one who founded a church for establishing and defending a just, virtuous and godly society.

It might well be said, then, that the Bible does not have just one clear political and social ethic. What it does is to make an unequivocal demand for justice and compassion in society, to insist on the highest standards of sincerity, honesty and unselfishness in public life, and to require that, whatever political system one supports, the poor and disadvantaged must always be considered with kindness and respect. These are values which give the Bible a vital and compelling relevance to social life, even though they allow Biblical Christians to hold a wide range of different political views.

Christians who try to base their moral views on the Bible will have to make many decisions as to how to interpret the texts, and how to derive conclusions in quite new areas that the Bible does not explicitly talk about. Some people will probably always hold to written rules in the New Testament. Others, equally Biblical in their approach, will take their clue from Paul's teaching that the written law kills, but the Spirit gives life (2 Corinthians 3:6). They will seek for the guidance of the Spirit in meeting new moral situations, and be prepared to amend particular rules in new contexts – just as the apostles amended the Torah in the early years of the church.

## SECOND VIEW: NATURAL LAW AS THE BASIS OF ETHICS

In the history of the Christian Church, moral teaching has in fact rarely been derived directly from the Biblical texts. It was always perceived that those texts were too complex and often provisional for that. The usual basis for Christian moral teaching, at least in the Catholic tradition, has been what is called 'Natural Law'. The Natural Law consists of those principles of morality which can be known without the aid of revelation, by the use of human reason alone. Thus the majority Christian view is that moral principles are knowable by reason, and do not depend for their truth or status upon religion. Nevertheless, God does make the moral law binding on humans, and can add things to it by revelation, without contradicting it.

Thomas Aquinas gave the classical formulation of Natural Law, in *Summa Theologiae* Question 94. It is based on the fact that God created the natural order, and thus on the belief that the inherent purposes of nature express the creative purpose of God. We humans know what these purposes are, by considering what the natural inclinations of living creatures are, since God has ordered our inclinations to their proper ends. So, for instance, all creatures have a natural inclination or tendency to preserve themselves, and to procreate. They have an inclination to live in groups, and, if they are rational, to seek knowledge and happiness.

On these simple God-given inclinations the whole of fundamental morality is founded. The natural inclination and purpose of living things is to preserve themselves, so the preservation of life is a natural good, a thing to be desired. Humans are rational agents who can direct their actions consciously in accordance with general principles, so we ought to preserve life wherever possible. It is natural and good for living organisms to procreate, so we ought to ensure that procreation is encouraged in the best possible conditions for the rearing of offspring. As rational animals, we seek to be sociable, knowledgeable and happy. No sane person would call these undesirable things. So it is just obviously right that we ought to pursue them as natural human goods.

All these principles are rather general, and need defining rather more closely. But what is important is that Christian morality is in this way founded on the natural desires of human beings. What is in general good is not something obscure and hard to find. It is something perfectly obvious to everyone, if they will only think about human nature. Morality is not some arbitrary dictate of God. It is the best way to fulfil human nature – which is, of course, created by God.

The basic principle of Catholic morality is that one should never avoidably frustrate a purpose of nature, and that one should seek to identify the purposes of the divinely created natural order and sustain them. At a very general level, this is not too difficult to do. The problems arise when one tries to get more specific. The basic problem, in a nutshell, is this: how far do particular and often very unusual contexts affect the general principles one may accept? There is probably no agreed answer to this question from natural reason alone. So at that point the Roman Catholic church appeals to the gift of the Holy Spirit, who is to lead the church into all truth, and who gives authority to interpret and define natural law to the magisterium, the teaching authority, of the church.

What happens now is that the duty to preserve life is limited, as an absolute rule, to the preservation of innocent human life, and the church teaches that there is an absolute prohibition on the taking of innocent human life. You cannot, for any reason, take an innocent human life (thus the ban on abortion and euthanasia). The duty to procreate is limited, for humans, to procreation within a monogamous marriage. All marital acts of sex must be open to the possibility of procreation (thus the ban on artificial means of contraception), but there must be no procreation outside marriage. In social affairs, the duty to be sociable is specified by principles like that of 'subsidiarity' (no higher authority should do what a lower authority is capable of doing), of property ownership, and of obedience to authority so long as it rules in accordance with natural justice or fairness. In this respect, it should be noted that the 'natural law' of justice, or fair play between roughly equal human beings, can often conflict with the positive laws of particular nation-states. In such cases, the church is brought into conflict with political authorities, and Christian morality can be used to criticise the laws of particular states – a view which has potentially radical political implications. Finally, the duty of seeking happiness is limited by the requirement to consider the common good, and by a reminder that the highest human happiness lies in loving and obeying God, not in transitory sensual pleasure.

The attraction of the Natural Law view is that it does not make morality depend too closely on the interpretation of revealed texts – morality is something knowable in principle by anyone. Its difficulty is that in fact Roman Catholics differ noticeably in some respects in their moral judgements from other people, and even from other Christians. It is therefore hard to hold that there really is one set of moral principles knowable by all rational agents. No doubt all rational agents could hold that it is good to preserve life, in general. But would all agree that only human lives are to be preserved, or that an innocent life cannot be taken under any circumstances, or that abortion is the taking of an innocent human life? Apparently not, so at such points the teaching authority of the church becomes of great importance.

The appeal to Natural Law in the Catholic tradition is based on the view that God has created the structures of nature basically in order as they are, so they must be preserved and never frustrated. But there would be many who would see the processes of nature, governed in large part as they are by forces of natural selection and random mutation, as not at all morally binding, or even morally acceptable, if we could change them. Why should we not frustrate a purpose of nature, if that purpose destroys human lives – as the 'purpose' of nature in creating volcanoes, or in generating cancer cells, does?

Traditional Catholic theologians will at this point distinguish between purposes of nature which are life-enhancing and those which are disordered and dysfunctional. It is the former which are to be preserved, not the latter. It is obvious, however, that the Catholic tradition at this point relies on appeal to revelation and authority, since it requires a belief in a good creator to believe that there are life-enhancing purposes in nature, which ought to be preserved. It requires the authoritative decision of the magisterium to determine that particular acts (say, contraception) frustrate purposes of nature. From the Catholic viewpoint, such appeals are entirely reasonable, since there is indeed a creator, and he has given authority to his church in matters of faith and morals.

The general result of this approach in the Catholic tradition has been a rather wide and humane conception of morality, as not confined to Christians or to Biblical revelation in a very narrow sense. Human welfare and social justice have always been taken as the basis of morality, and major traditions of legal and political thought have arisen from the practice of casuistry (applying general principles to particular cases). The Catholic church has always proclaimed the sanctity of innocent human life, the inviolability of marriage, the importance of a stable home in which children can be brought up, and the necessity of governments which work for the common good, under the authority of a God of justice and mercy.

Natural Law thinking readily leads into the formulation of natural or universal human rights, because natural law lays down the duties that everyone owes to everyone else. My rights are those things that every other person has a duty to leave me in possession of, as far as possible – my life, my property and my freedom. Thus Catholic social teaching places a high priority on human rights, stressing that we must allow all humans the fundamental rights of dignity, respect, freedom and life, because God lays the duty of respecting them on everyone.

Catholics often tend to support conservative and hierarchical forms of government, partly because the church itself is seen as a conservative and hierarchical institution, which has historically found itself under severe attack from atheistic forms of Communism and Socialism. Yet it does not defend privilege and the oppression of the poor, precisely because it is bound to uphold the importance of universal human rights, which require respect and consideration for all humans, whatever their social position. And sometimes Catholic social thinking can be very radical, as with the development of Liberation theology in Latin America. After the conference of Latin American bishops at Medellin in 1968, major criticisms were made of the institutionalised violence of the rich against the poor. Taking a lead from the liberation of Israel from Egypt by God, and from Jesus' care for the socially outcast, Liberation theologians like Gustavo Gutierrez insisted that God's activity could be found principally amongst the poor, and called the church to work for the transformation of the structures of society.

So Catholic social thought usually stands between Communism, with its denial of the right of private ownership (and therefore, it would be said, of personal responsibility and stewardship), and unrestrained Capitalism, with its creation of a permanent underclass of the poor. It tries to balance a concern for universal human welfare with the right to create and preserve wealth in freedom. In the twentieth century it has moved noticeably away from more hierarchical political ideas towards a careful exploration of the sorts of social principles which could enable all human beings to flourish equitably, as equally loved children of God.

Overall, one might say that Catholic moral thought tends to be very conservative on matters of sexuality (sex is permitted only within monogamous marriage, for the primary purpose of procreation) and potentially subversive on matters of political theory (Aquinas said that an unjust law is no law, and need not be obeyed). In the modern world it is in a position to insist on consideration for justice throughout the world, and especially for those in the developing world, and to protest against abuse and violence to the human person in so many states. If its sexual proclamations seem to be honoured more in the breach than in their observance, its social and political witness is one which helps to make the modern world more humane and respectful of human rights. It calls for the flourishing of human nature and the establishment of true justice and peace in the world, so that all people can be free, responsible agents in communities of mutual support and concern. That is the enduring strength of the Catholic moral tradition.

## THIRD VIEW: PERSONALISM AS THE BASIS OF ETHICS

Nevertheless, many Christians feel uneasy about the Natural Law tradition, at least as it has been traditionally interpreted. Partly this is because of a certain scepticism about authoritative moral statements made by the church in the past. For instance, vaccination was condemned as against Natural Law, and death was accepted as a punishment for heresy. The ban on artificial methods of contraception is widely ignored, and many Christians doubt whether there is any clear Biblical precedent for giving one institutional body the power to give infallible moral teaching.

More seriously, the tradition sometimes seems to adopt a rather 'biological' interpretation of Natural Law, according to which sex, for example, exists only for the purpose of procreation. Clearly, in one sense sex does exist for that purpose. But in human beings the biological structure is overlaid by more personal considerations. It may be thought that the body exists for the sake of the soul, or person, and not that the person must always conform to the normal processes of the body. So between human persons sexual union expresses a deeper personal union; it expresses love. Can it not be properly used to express love, even when there has been a principled decision not to procreate children at a particular time? Further, why should the pleasure in sexual union not be valued for its own sake, even if procreation is not possible or intended?

So some Christians would adopt a more personalist approach to morality. They agree with the Natural Law tradition that the natural order is the creation of a good God, who has specific purposes in creation. But they identify those purposes rather differently. One of the chief purposes of God, they would say, is that the cosmos should generate, out of its material processes, rational persons who can create, in co-operation with God, communities of justice and love. It follows that, in general, what conduces to such communities, and to personal flourishing within them, is good, and what frustrates them is bad.

So far there is no disagreement. But then one comes to ask exactly what is conducive to personal flourishing and human community. Is it conformity to the processes of nature as such, or is it sometimes a shaping of the processes of nature towards a greater degree of personal flourishing? In the case of contraception, for instance, persons might flourish better in a world with not vastly too many people in it, where all children could be cared for responsibly and with proper attention, and where parents would not be afraid to have marital intercourse in case they have more children. One of the greatest perils of the modern world is over-population, and one of the tragedies of human life is the large number of teenage pregnancies, producing abortions or unwanted babies who cannot be properly cared for. In a world like this, it seems obvious to many Christians that God would wish humans to bear children responsibly and carefully, having regard for their proper upbringing and welfare. At the same time, there is little reason to forbid sexual union, which brings pleasure and expresses love, if means can be found to make it possible while preventing undesired pregnancy.

Some Christians might feel that God wills as many souls as possible to be created, or that God plans the birth of every soul, and we should not frustrate that plan. But others will feel that the welfare of those souls which do exist is more important than the generation of as many souls as possible (or at least the refusal to frustrate their possible generation). They will feel it is wholly unrealistic to limit acts of marital union to occasions on which conception is not artificially prevented. And they will feel that the role of chance and accident at a biological level, where a great many mutations are harmful, is such that one cannot suppose that God wills everything to happen just as it does.

Deep issues are touched on here, but one simple way of putting the point is to say that traditional moralists hold that one should not frustrate the purposes of nature, while personalists deny that there are any *moral* purposes in nature itself. God has purposes in creating nature, but nature is still in the process of being shaped, and contains many random and accidental occurrences, many things that do not happen for the best. So we best forward God's purposes by shaping nature in accordance with the intention of helping persons to flourish. This will sometimes mean frustrating biological processes, when they themselves impede human flourishing. We should not hesitate to destroy cancer cells, however natural their growth is, biologically. In a similar way, we should not hesitate to destroy an embryo whose coming to term will certainly kill both mother and child.

Some of the most difficult moral issues arise in the quite new situation where we are in a position to alter the genetic make-up of human beings. To what extent should we design the genetic structure to produce specific sorts of human beings, eliminate genetic defects, or enhance specific inherited characteristics? There is a natural fear of changing the biological basis of human beings, but one has to ask whether this is a fear of impinging on structures which God has laid down, or whether it is a fear of producing consequences as yet unforeseen.

Personalists would probably say that, since the natural order produces many extremely harmful mutations and hereditary diseases (like leukemia), it is irresponsible to leave nature as it is, when we have the power to change it. The effects of grave hereditary disorders are so bad that if we can eliminate or replace genes which cause them, it is our duty to do so. The possibilities of unforeseen harm in such cases seem smaller than the demonstrable harm which would be averted. However, attempts positively to select for good characteristics (like high intelligence) do not carry enough clear benefit to outweigh the unforeseen harms which genetic engineering might carry. The prudent course might well seem to be to permit negative genetic screening to eliminate clear genetic defects, where possible, but to prohibit positive genetic selection until much more has been discovered about the function of specific genes in human growth and development.

Even in suggesting this cautious approach, however, one would have moved beyond the stage of prohibiting medical intervention just because it frustrates a natural process. One would be encouraging the shaping of natural processes to purposes which could be identified as good by the help of the revelation of human excellence in Christ, and which nature might itself frustrate. The personalist would have moved beyond the 'law of nature', to consider how nature might serve the purposes of personal flourishing.

Other crucial areas of disagreement between traditionalists and personalists are those of life and death and sexual practice. Of course personalists will believe that human life is created in God's image, and so is worthy of special respect. They will support every effort to preserve life and prevent its destruction. But they may hold that there are closely circumscribed borderline cases where even innocent human life, or potentially human life, can be taken. One might be when a terribly injured person, soon about to die, and in great pain, begs to be killed. Another might be when a young girl has been raped and has become pregnant, when it becomes clear that she and the growing embryo cannot both survive. A third might be when a soldier is, under torture, about to divulge information that will result in the deaths of thousands of his compatriots.

These are all very difficult moral cases, and it is easy to see why people are perplexed about them, since they bring differing, equally strong, moral intuitions into conflict. The personalist will not offer an easy solution, but may maintain that it is not satisfactory just to lay down an absolute prohibition on the taking of innocent human life, as though that settles the issue. Similarly, while lying and stealing are undoubtedly wrong in general, there may be cases where it becomes right to lie or steal – in order to save lives, for example. The moral map is perhaps just a little more hazy than moral absolutists suppose. But that does not mean there are no clear contours or commanding heights at all.

As in the case of the other two approaches to Christian social morality, Christian personalists do not necessarily agree on some specific political agenda. They would clearly favour social systems which encourage a concern for universal human welfare, and would probably place a high value on personal liberty, on equality of treatment, and on the possibility of democratic participation in decision-making processes. But there may be different ways in which it is appropriate to seek such things, depending on the historical and social context in which one lives. In a country oppressed by military or economic forces, one might concentrate on the need to free the oppressed and give them a real say in the structure of society. While in a rich and free country where people are able to pursue their own pleasure in many diverse ways, one might focus more on creating institutions to reinforce stable families, or on programmes to make people aware of their responsibilities to less developed parts of the world. The general ideals and the limits of morally permissible action would be clear, but specific ways of implementing them might be reasonably disputed between Christians, as they are disputed between people of good will in general. In other words, both Socialists and Conservatives can be good Christians, as long as they genuinely try to maximise human freedom for all, and to eliminate poverty and undeserved inequality so far as possible from society.

In matters of human sexuality, if the Christian position is that biological relationships should always be subordinated to the expression of fidelity and love between persons, and if it is not felt to be a sin to express sexuality without always holding open the possibility of procreation, then long-term homosexual relationships are permissible, and could well be conducive to the personal flourishing of those of same-sex orientation. Sexual relationships outside marriage are commonplace in modern societies, and the church may want to explore new ways of relating these to considerations of fidelity and loyalty, rather than simply to declare them forbidden.

For traditional Christians, all this might be seen as 'giving in' to the secular world. But it might also be seen as an adjustment to new social, economic and biological possibilities, in order to preserve the crucial values of personal flourishing and community in a rapidly changing world. For holders of this third view, Christian morality is more of an exploratory, less rule-bound activity. Its guiding principle is not, 'Keep the rules unbroken', but rather, 'Explore (but with great care and sensitivity) new ways of encouraging personal flourishing in a community of mutual concern'. After all, it was Jesus who rejected strict and traditional religious interpretations of moral rules, and said, 'The Sabbath was made for man, not man for the Sabbath' (Mark 2:27). This is the motto for those who see Christian morality as an adventure into love, in which compassion and kindness have a greater part to play than insistence on rigorous conformity to laws, whatever the situation.

So Christians appeal to the Bible, to church traditional teaching, and to personal experience of the demands of love in a changing world, to various degrees and in various ways. Underlying all the sharp differences on particular issues like contraception, abortion and sexuality there is an unfaltering agreement that God is love, that God wills human beings to experience and express love, and that love requires a respect and compassion for others which is not restricted by race or creed. For all our perplexities about exactly what love requires, these are foundations which keep Christians committed to universal compassion as an ultimate moral value, and to the vital importance of the search for it. Christians are unequivocally committed to the importance and truth of a morality of self-giving love. Christianity places a central emphasis on the importance of an unwavering commitment to justice and to human flourishing, together with an insistence that human moral failures call for compassion and forgiveness rather than for judgement and condemnation, and an acknowledgement that we can never rest content with our own moral achievements. In these ways Christianity has played an important part in the development of moral insight and understanding in the modern world.

# 14 CHRISTIANITY AND CULTURE

C hristianity has affected the shape and character of morality, and so had a major effect on the cultures in which it has existed. It has also given a distinctive shape and impetus to the development of literature, art, music and science. The Bible itself is a great work of literature, containing stories and poems as well as histories and law-codes. It is said that the Spirit of God inspired David to write the psalms, and Bezalel to design the Temple of God. So the power of story, the beauty of poetry and song, and the splendour of sculptured wood and stone, were associated with Hebrew religion from its first recorded days. Jesus was brought up on the poetry of the psalms, and he taught in unforgettable aphorisms and stories of piercing insight. His recorded sayings show an awareness and love of the natural world of seed-time and harvest. He celebrated the annual Festivals, with their choreographed ritual and colourful decoration. He was said to be a carpenter, shaping with his own hands objects (one assumes!) of elegant design. The patterning of visual and aural stim-uli into complexes which provoke insight, emotion and the sense of transcendent beauty – in a word, the arts – were always closely asso-ciated with religion in the Biblical world. Similarly, the natural world and the starry sky are always seen in the Bible as showing the awe-some and beautiful craftsmanship of God, and the pursuit of wisdom and understanding is a proper part of the praise of God.

Nevertheless, the relationship between Christianity and the arts and sciences has not always been straightforward. In keeping with the general plan of this book, three main types of relationship can be distinguished, though in the account which follows I shall adopt a generally chronological narrative in which these three types will to a large extent overlap. The first type of relationship is that in which the arts and sciences are subordinated to the aims and values of Christianity. The faith seeks to express itself in architecture, painting, music and literature, but tries to ensure that these forms are suitable for Christian expression, and so exercises a sort of control or censorship over the arts. Christianity built the first universities in Europe, and always encouraged the pursuit of astronomy and of the study of the natural world. But it often tried to ensure that scientific activity remained firmly under its own control. The best known example is probably the placing of Galileo under house arrest by the Catholic Church in the sixteenth century – though that was due more to a conflict between Aristotelian and Copernican astronomy than to any essential conflict between astronomy and the church. In the present day, some Protestants still reject the theory of evolution because they hold it to be inconsistent with the teaching of the Bible. So attempts are sometimes made to ensure that science conforms to religious doctrines which are known in advance.

The second type of relationship is one in which Christians reject most forms of external expression, prohibiting images, icons, elaborate buildings and music, and works of imaginative fiction. All is centred on austere and inward worship in simplicity, and service to the poor replaces expenditure on glittering buildings. In science, some Christians may simply regard the empirical study of nature as lacking religious point. In the fourteenth century there were those who regarded experimental investigations as intruding on the mysteries of God, and perhaps an echo of this is found in some modern statements that genetic manipulation is taking on the prerogatives of God. The arts may well respond in an exaggerated way by attacking Christianity as a joyless and negative way of life, and the sciences have tended to respond equally one-sidedly by calling religion a mass of vain superstitions.

The third type of relationship is one for which art develops quite separately from religion, and sometimes becomes a replacement for Christianity, cultivating an aesthetic religiosity, perhaps in the love of nature or reverential attendance at musical gatherings. The sciences, too, can generate an ersatz religion, and the manner in which some Darwinians propagate their faith with evangelical fervour is unmistakably reminiscent of religion, with its own rigorously maintained creed and its priesthood of true believers. Christian faith can, however, use such autonomously developed arts and sciences to express its own ideals, and indeed to reshape its ideals to some extent in the light of new artistic creations and scientific discoveries. All three attitudes have been found in Christian history, so that the relationship between Christianity and culture is a many-sided but usually creative one for both.

## FIRST VIEW: ART AND SCIENCE IN THE SERVICE OF FAITH

In the first centuries of Christianity, the major artistic activity was the building of churches and cathedrals. As early as the end of the fourth century, Christians began to build basilicas, modelled on Roman law-courts, to house the relics of martyrs and to provide spaces in which increasingly elaborate liturgies could be enacted. From about the twelfth century the great cathedrals of Europe took form as gigantic testimonies in stone and glass to the power and grandeur of the creator and of his church. Filled with symbolism, they were usually cruciform in shape, with a High Altar at the East end, Biblical scenes depicted in windows and on painted walls, and high vaulted ceilings and spires reaching towards heaven. As the Pyramids expressed the ancient Egyptian fascination with death, and the Pharaoh's hope for immortality, so the great Christian cathedrals form a sacred space in which people gather in community to celebrate the mysteries of the coming of God among the people to re-present his self-sacrifice for their well-being. This space is a sacramental space – not primarily for the celebration of private devotions or for the worship of images, and not primarily for social gatherings. The space is a meeting point of heaven and earth, where the creator offers the medicine of immortality, and where the people are taken into the divine life.

In Eastern Orthodox churches, the iconostasis, a sacred screen covered with icons, keeps the celebration of the holy mystery of the Eucharist apart from the congregation, who move among the candles and sacred icons, from whence, when the great doors of the screen are opened, they see the consecrated elements elevated in procession, and receive blessed bread to symbolise their participation in the heavenly mystery. There is an objectivity about the liturgy. It goes on with its own efficacy, and the members of the congregation come and go, walking around and talking as well as joining in the singing or chants. There is a sense that this is something God does, in which the people may participate in varying degrees, and the physical building becomes the place wherein the saving activity of God is made present to the local community. The emphasis tends to be on the incarnating and healing Christ, the one who sanctifies matter and who gives grace, usually in and through the intercession of the saints and especially of the Blessed Virgin his mother, to heal the sins of those who ask for pardon.

In the Roman Catholic church, too, the celebration of the Mass traditionally took place at a High Altar, far removed from the congregation, with the priests facing away from them towards the altar. Ornate vestments and elaborate music, incense and candlelight, with sunlight channelled through long narrow windows, increased the sense of awe and mystery. At the moment of consecration, a bell would ring, the priests would kneel, and all would adore the God made flesh. The central symbol is of God coming to the people in material form, though always in mystery and remote splendour. However, on great occasions, and more often for the devout, the people would move near to the altar to eat the sacred bread and wine, and receive the life of God into their very selves.

The emphasis in the Latin, Western tradition is more on the Cross, on the sacrifice of Christ. Since the eleventh century, crucifixes have been commonplace in Latin churches, and they emphasise the suffering of Christ because of the sins of the world. Latin churches do not usually contain icons, but they contain statues, especially of the Blessed Virgin Mary, and stained-glass windows, which provide representations of the sacred etched in light. There will normally be a number of shrines of saints, and every altar will contain some relics of a saint. There is room for private devotions at many side chapels, even though the central ritual is that of the great High Mass, with full public pomp and ceremony. There is, however, the same hierarchical flowing of grace down from bishop to priest to congregation, physically symbolised by the bishop's throne, the priests' location by the altar, and the people's proper place in the body of the church.

So the great cathedrals of East and West are centres of sacred, hierarchically controlled power, a power given to form disciples into a community who live by the forgiveness and grace of God. This is an understanding of the Christian way which can seem alien to many Christians. Protestants, especially, may be embarrassed by the sometimes ostentatious magnificence of the great cathedrals, and their presentation of worship as something that goes on whether or not a congregation is present, or really participates in it. Both Calvin and Luther wished to have a greater stress on the simplicity of Christian life and worship, on the need for participation by all the faithful, and on the necessity for a conscious understanding and acceptance of the Word of God by the faithful. Protestant churches tend to be less splendid, architecturally, and to be without icons or statues. They have their own beauty and simplicity, but they rarely have the baroque ornateness and splendour of the Mediterranean Catholic cathedrals. There is less stress on visual symbols of faith, and emphasis is placed instead on the Word of the Bible and preaching based upon it. The pulpit is placed prominently, sometimes higher than the altar. The idea of an altar is often replaced by that of a 'Holy Table', where the Lord's Supper can be celebrated with simplicity, and on special occasions. Since the invention of organs, these have been prominent in all Western churches, and so Protestant faith tends to be a religion of sound rather than of sight; of public hearing, praying and singing rather than of private devotion; of an inner simplicity of heart rather than of the cultic evocation of a sense of mystery and awe.

Protestant Christians are suspicious of statues because of the Biblical prohibition of the making of 'carved images' (Exodus 20:4). But in contrast to Hebrew art, where the depiction of the deity was, at least officially, forbidden, Christians have used representational pictures of sacred things from very early times. The Hebrew Bible forbids making 'carved images', and some have taken this to forbid any representational art at all. The Christian view was changed by reflection on the fact that Jesus was believed to be 'the image of the invisible God', the historical expression of the eternal God. Since God had taken human form, it must be permissible to depict that form in art. Such depiction could serve to make God's presence more clearly known, and be a reminder that the material world could indeed express spiritual reality.

There are pictures of Jesus, often as a young beardless shepherd or as seated in glory, from tombs of the third and fourth centuries. In the Eastern church, Jesus, Mary and the saints were regularly depicted in paintings or sculptures, and again the emphasis was upon the youth and vitality of Christ, or upon his existence in glory, and his ability to give eternal life to his devotees. There was little stress on the crucifixion, certainly not as a terrible or bloody event. In the seventh and eighth centuries 'iconoclasts' in the Eastern churches opposed the veneration of icons, and saw them as forms of idolatry. But, after many disputes, in 843 a Council of the Eastern Churches announced the 'Triumph of Orthodoxy', when icons were definitively accepted as proper objects of reverence. Since that time icons have become essential parts of the celebration of the liturgy in the East.

Icons express the sacredness, or at least the potential sacredness, of the created order, and give rise to a sense of visual art as conveying knowledge of transcendent spiritual reality. In time the conventions governing the painting of icons became very strict, so that although there was a strong sense of the transparency of matter to the sacred, the forms in which this could be allowed to occur were relatively restricted, and kept under church control. This in turn led to a fairly strong distinction developing between sacred and secular art. Where institutional authority tries to censor works of art to ensure that they express the 'correct' moral or religious significance, there is a danger of stifling real artistic creativity. On the other hand, the authorities are aware that artistic creativity can be used to express depravity and decadence (as in pornography or sado-masochism) as well as beauty. The balance is a hard one to achieve, and in the Orthodox world the decision has been to insist on the maintenance of tradition in religious art.

## SECOND VIEW: ART AND SCIENCE BEGIN TO SEPARATE FROM FAITH

In the Western Roman Empire, once a relative stability was achieved between warring tribal groups, there was a more volatile and restless attitude to the arts. The European Renaissance, when it came in the late fourteenth century, saw the birth of a new fusion of the ancient classical Greek and Roman ideals of art with Christian themes of spirituality. There was a movement in art from the stylised abstraction of iconic portraiture towards a more dynamic, flowing and realistic depiction of human life. The themes were largely still religious, and the pictures filled with religious symbolism, but there was a much greater emphasis on the human, and a feeling that Christian faith must be placed within the cultural tradition of a recovered love of the human world.

This was exactly the task that the fourth- and fifth-century theologians had undertaken when they formulated Christian doctrines in Greek, largely Platonic terminology. But those doctrines, radical and innovative in their day, had become ossified into irreformable dogmas, just as iconic art had settled largely into repetitions of formulaic designs. Now, in Holland and even more in Italy, there was a rebirth of art, literature and music. Earlier artistic traditions had sought to make earthly forms into images of the spiritual, abstracting from their particular humanity so as to make the spiritual present to the senses. Now, in the Renaissance, artists sought to make spiritual things fully embodied in the human. The works of Fra Angelico and Botticelli replace the rather impersonal icons of tradition with recognisable individual faces and figures, arranged in the poses of classical humanism. Christian humanism was born out of a fusion of the classical delight in particular form with the Christian belief in the supernatural destiny of things precisely in their individuality. The spiritual was not seen as something opposed to the material, to be gained by a denial of all sensory delights. The material was not seen as the only place where beauty might be found, fleetingly and by the cultured few. Rather, the human world in all its particularity was seen as a place of infinite value, because it was taken into the divine life. The temporal was eternalised, just as the human nature of Jesus had been transfigured by being assumed into the divine life. For such a vision of the world, humanism does not conflict with faith. On the contrary, it is the work of faith not to despise but to revere the human as the apotheosis of the particular, celebrated for the unique reality and fulfilment that God intends it to have.

As in painting, so in the literature of Dante, Petrarch and Boccaccio, and in the works of Chaucer and Shakespeare, one can detect a liberation of creative thought from what had come to be felt as the restrictive confines of church authority. These voices were certainly not deferential to, or even very interested in, ecclesiastical structures and pronouncements. They celebrate the goodness of the sensory world, though they are keenly aware of its ambiguity and tragedy. There is unmistakably a shift of focus towards the human and the importance of the individual. But that shift does not renounce the transcendent dimension. Human life is viewed as a drama of high moral earnestness, a battle of good and evil, and an internal struggle with a basically good but deeply flawed human nature. There is a celebration of individuality, a fear of judgement, and a hope for some sort of victory of the good. Humanity is escaping from an age of centralised institutional authority, but it is repristinating a vision of human life touched by a transcendent dimension, a vision of divinity incarnate, hidden yet disclosed in the attentive creativity of poets and painters.

This vision goes back to the very beginnings of the Christian era. The four Gospels, while they are certainly meant to be founded on facts of history, could well be seen as novels, so well constructed and poignantly depicted are the events of Jesus' life and passion which they record. Narrative is the form of the Old Testament stories of the Patriarchs, the form in which Jesus' life is told, the form in which Jesus so often taught. It has become characteristic of Christian culture that the deepest truths of human existence should be disclosed in story – not in fantastical stories of mythical realms of the gods or primordial beings, but in stories of ordinary human lives which are somehow touched by a dimension of transcendence. What Christianity suggests, in its doctrine that the divine was incarnate in a human form, is that the mundane and the sacred are not divided. The mundane, when it exists as it should, is the vehicle of the sacred. Yet its evident incapacity to carry such a weight is the source of the tragic vision which marks so much Christian literature.

Some have held that there cannot be a tragic Christian vision, because everything has a happy ending, and so forms a 'Divine Comedy'. But the tragedy lies in the failure of creation to be what it could and should be, the sense of the loss of what might have been, the knowledge of suffering caused to the innocent by the carelessness or callousness of the selfish. Some goods can never be regained, and even at the restoration of all things for which Christians look there will always be the memory of the scars of that suffering which human sin has caused.

So literature which has been informed by Christian thinking has exposed the self-destructive circle of greed and hatred in human life, and its desperate search for a way out. Much European literature, like that of Sartre and Camus, has opposed institutional religion itself, as a false way out. But it has analysed the human situation in a way deeply consistent with the Christian view. It has even shared the hostility to the authorities of established religion which was so marked in the life of Jesus, who was, after all, killed at the request of the religious establishment. It has also often perceived the paradoxical salvation which love and compassion offers in a world otherwise condemned to futility.

One might say that images of the Fall and of the Cross have loomed larger, in European literature, than images of the Resurrection and of Eternal Life. Partly that is because, as Dostoevsky said, goodness is so very difficult to depict. It is also, perhaps, because of the very this-worldliness of incarnational Christianity that the 'other world' of resurrection and eternity is so difficult to portray. All one can show is hints of such a world, shafts of ambiguous light in the darkness. Just as we do not know exactly what Jesus' resurrection was like, so we do not know just what human resurrection will be like. So literature speaks more of redemptive love, of the power of self-sacrifice, of an imperfect but obstinate hope for some human fulfilment. In Shakespeare's *King Lear*, Dostoevsky's *The Brothers Karamazov*, and in Camus' *The Plague*, love is seen as a redemptive force, but the full experience of redemption is hidden, even uncertain.

This reflects the fact that Jesus died on the Cross with forgiveness on his lips, and with a great cry. But what followed no longer belonged to history in the objective sense, and can be grasped only by the inward experience of faith. The classical literature of Christian cultures does not depict the certainty of further lives beyond death, and does not depict miraculous activities of the gods in the world of men and women. It rather depicts the fragilities and failures of human life, and yet the fascination and unique individuality of humans, in their irreplaceable personal being. It accepts that there is an intense moral conflict at the heart of human existence, and that moral decisions are made with infinite passion. And it tends to suggest a sort of forgiveness, or a possibility of contrition, or at the least a possibility of reconciliation in the midst of human fragility. Such reconciliation is rarely wholly successful, yet an underlying belief in human dignity and an underlying hope for goodness – perhaps, one might say, even for a redemption which humans cannot themselves accomplish, but which may be given to them – is present, expressed precisely by the intense interest in individuality which belief in the human soul has bequeathed to the post-Christian literary world.

Christianity has given a certain tone to literature – this-worldly, interested in individuality, intensely aware of fragility and estrangement, conscious of the rigorous centrality of moral choice, ambiguously touched by moments of transcendence, and desiring a redemption which will not destroy the world as it is, but may in some unimaginable way transform it. This mood is at its clearest in the plays of Goethe and Shakespeare, and in the novels of Dickens – not overtly pious or religious works, but filled with a sense of the moral tragedy and sublimity of human existence, and of the elusively transcendent character of human nature. Even the more overtly religious works of Dante and Milton express a fascination with human individuality, and the poetry of the Romantics endues Nature itself with qualities of spiritual presence. So in European literature the impact of Christianity is felt not so much in writings with an explicitly religious theme, as in loving attention to the human world as a place where spiritual reality is hidden in the everyday. It is the idea of Incarnation, of the concealment of Spirit in the material world, that has touched the literary imagination of Europe.

With the invention of the printing press in 1455, literature became available to a much wider public, and new translations of the Bible were produced – eighteen of them in Germany alone in the fifteenth century. To the austere beauty of the Latin Mass and the monastic Offices was now added a rendering of the Word of God in a hundred different languages. Sometimes, as with the English King James' Bible, a beauty of language was achieved (even if by a committee of rather inaccurate translators) which has never been surpassed. Hymns and devotional works were written, and religious faith found expression in literary forms which spoke to the hearts of men and women. It was natural to set such words to music, and from the sixteenth century onwards church music, both Catholic and Protestant, developed rapidly in its exploration of new harmonies, carrying new and powerful emotional resonances.

In the Middle Ages, the art of choral and polyphonic singing developed out of the daily recitation of the psalms, and the liturgy of the Eucharist. In the West, this sort of church music reached its apogee with Palestrina, whose austere yet complex harmonies, setting a traditional Latin text to a calm, flowing continuum of interwoven vocal lines still to many people epitomises what 'spiritual music' is. The mood is contemplative and serene, with a beautiful clarity of line, and a range of texts set by the Christian liturgy. For some people, a Palestrina Mass performed in a Gothic cathedral, surrounded by paintings and sculptures of the Italian masters, with the full ceremony of the solemn liturgy, conveys the heart of Christianity. Yet one cannot ignore the fact that for others (like Bernard of Clairvaux, the twelfth-century saint who wrote to Abbot William of St Thierry, 'O vanity of vanities ... the church glitters on every side, but the poor are hungry') all this is a betrayal of the simplicity of faith, and a misuse of money that could be given to the poor.

## THIRD VIEW: ART AND SCIENCE AS ALTERNATIVES TO FAITH

With the dawn of the European Enlightenment, the controversy between those who wished to deploy the arts in the service of faith, and those who saw the arts as an expensive deflection from the simple worship of the heart and the service of the poor, was reconfigured by historical events. The church attempted to control the forms of painting and music that were appropriate to religion (rather as Plato had recommended confining poetry and music to suitably uplifting themes). But the arts developed their own autonomous cultural life. There is no more profoundly felt music anywhere than J.S. Bach's *St Matthew Passion*, or Handel's *Messiah*. The theme of Christ's life and passion are given a musical embodiment which evokes a rarely surpassed emotional depth. But those composers also wrote dances, operas and secular suites. While Mozart, Haydn and Beethoven wrote great religious works, they are better known for their symphonies, works without particular religious significance. Music, like literature and painting, was becoming distinct from religion, pursuing its own patterns and styles, revelling in the creation of harmony and of the organic development of form for its own sake.

New developments in musical form, a greater attention to secular themes in art, and the rise of sceptical philosophical views, signalled a growing separation from religious life. Yet the seventeenth and eighteenth centuries in Europe still held to a background belief that the world was the product of one rational creator. Isaac Newton, one of the greatest originators of modern science, and a pious Christian of a Unitarian frame of mind, claimed to read in the 'Book of Nature' the laws that God had laid down from eternity. There was a faith, or confidence, that the world, being rationally structured, could be understood by reason, and indeed that Christianity itself was at heart a wholly reasonable faith. It had, after all, been responsible for the foundation of the first European universities, and the church encouraged the development of scientific understanding of the universe. Much has sometimes been made of the controversies that occurred between Galileo and the Catholic Church, or between Darwin and some Christian thinkers. But of course the churches had their own observatories, astronomers, laboratories and biologists, and those were controversies that occurred quite properly between scientists of differing views. Of more importance is the Christian belief in the free creation of the universe by a rational God (or through a rational principle, the Logos), so that the universe is an intelligible yet contingent whole which can be rationally understood by minds made in the image of God. That belief made empirical science possible, and Christian scientists like Newton and Mendel have been at the forefront of those who have made major discoveries in physics, astronomy and biology, for example. So, while there have been controversies and arguments, as there always are and properly should be, in a lively and creative intellectual life, the progress of science in the last three centuries has been largely inspired by a Christian vision of an intelligible, beautiful and ordered universe, and by a feeling that we should seek to understand more fully a universe which has been shaped by divine wisdom. In the late seventeenth century, the optimistic vision of a rational universe open to progressive human understanding marked the philosophy of Locke and Leibniz, and the science of Isaac Newton. If there was some uncertainty about some of the more mysterious elements of traditional Christianity (like the Trinity, the Incarnation and the Mass), there continued to be a deep faith in the doctrine of rational creation.

But European society was also shaken by the wars of religion between Catholic and Protestant, and by a growing surge of feeling against the privilege and inherited wealth of the *ancien régime*, which culminated in the French Revolution. Reason, when employed to its fullest extent, even seemed to undermine its own credentials. Kant's *Critique of Pure Reason*, in 1781, argued that Reason leads to unavoidable contradictions when pressed beyond its proper employment in the realm of sense-experience. Hegel, who thought of himself rather oddly as the first Christian philosopher, proceeded to see the contradictions of Reason as a clue to the nature of a reality which could not be comprehended by human Understanding, but required a higher form of rational intuition to grasp. The Romantic movement in music and literature led to a stage at which art became itself a form of religion. In the beauties of the natural world, portrayed in dramatic landscapes of breathtaking mountains and storm-filled skies, in poetry which evoked a sense of the infinite in the finite forms of flowers and hills, and in the emotionally overwhelming symphonic poems and music-dramas of Richard Strauss and Richard Wagner, the arts left behind the dogmas of Christianity, and became themselves the gateway to transcendent spiritual experience and the sense of the numinous.

The religion of art produced few saints and few scholars. Its dangers became clear in the misuse of Wagner's music to support the

activities of the German National Socialists. The sense of the numinous, of a mystic wholeness and a union with nature, blood and soil,
all too easily became confused with subservience to the 'Spirit of the
People', and an alliance with the natural forces of the will to power
and survival, which Darwin and Marx had so starkly highlighted.
Christianity, it would seem, still has something to give to art. That is
not to confine it to the rules of timid convention, and not to oppose
it as unwanted luxury, but to encourage artists to seek to evoke a
transcendent depth in finite forms, and to inform understanding of
that depth by the self-giving compassion of Jesus and the wisdom of
the Spirit which gives pattern, form and order to all things.

Perhaps Christianity has something important to give to the scientific understanding of the universe, too. There is a danger that the
search for understanding may endanger the moral constraints which
enjoin respect for life, and bring the planet itself into mortal danger.
There is a Faustian search for knowledge uncontrolled by moral wisdom, which offers power over nature, but without ethical responsibility. What Christian wisdom can contribute is a sense of the value
of personal life, and of all things insofar as they enhance God's creation. It can reinforce the sense that science is a search for wisdom,
to be used for the welfare of living beings, and for the integrity and
health of a creation which is intended, with human help, to express
the being and beauty of God. And it can counter the sense of mean-
inglessness and disillusionment which can overtake those who see the
universe as just the result of chance and blind necessity, by reminding
them of the purpose and providence of God in creation.

The arts and sciences are certainly no longer under the control of any
institutional church. But the Christian churches are committed to
evoking signs of the wisdom, beauty and love of God in the natural
world, by encouraging people to shape its sounds and sights to
delight the ear and eye, and raise the mind to the creator who is the
source of all beauty and intelligibility. As Christianity has spread from
Byzantium and the Western Roman Empire throughout the world, so

many diverse cultures – not only the European – will surely inspire new insights into the manifold beauties potential in the created universe. Christian art, literature, music and science is bound to be much more globally and indeed cosmically oriented in future. Christianity will be freer in its use of metaphor and imagery, seeking to encourage forms of art that enable one, in William Blake's words, to 'hold infinity in the palm of a hand, and eternity in an hour'. Both arts and sciences are expressions of the creative human spirit. Insofar as that spirit is informed by the Spirit of creative love which formed the universe, and which is seen by Christians as disclosed in a new and more personal form in Jesus, Christian art and science will continue to have a distinctive role as an attempt to co-operate with the creativity of the divine Spirit in ever-new ways of shaping the forms of the material cosmos.

# 15 PRAYER

I have considered the effect of Christianity on morality, and on the arts and sciences. While there have been many varying forms of relationship between them, there can be little doubt that the influence of Christianity has been a deeply creative and inspirational one. Perhaps some people would value Christianity for its moral teaching, its artistic achievements, and its encouragement of scientific understanding alone. But the heart of Christianity is prayer, the conscious relationship of thought and feeling to God. Christian prayer can take the three main forms of public worship, personal devotion, and silent contemplation. So there are three main views of the nature of prayer, though there is no reason why they should not co-exist and complement one another, and indeed they normally do.

## FIRST VIEW: LITURGY

Human thoughts are expressed in language which is learned from others, and feelings are shaped and directed by response to others. Thus prayer is naturally and primarily a public activity, by which one learns and develops ways of addressing God and ways of responding to God in various situations. It would be unwise to try to begin just for oneself to find appropriate ways to address God, when generations of Christians have practised this art together. In particular, many communities of Christians have sought to live out their relationship to God by a daily round of public prayer and worship. The traditions thereby built up have become known as the public prayer, or liturgy, of the church, by which God is praised throughout each day, and by which the church, as the body of Christ, is related to its Head, its Sustainer, and its Goal.

In monasteries seven 'Offices' or services of prayer developed, in accordance with the Biblical statement, 'seven times a day do I praise thee' (Psalm 119:164). These consist of reciting the Psalms and other parts of the Bible. The whole of the Biblical Psalms are recited regularly, usually by singing alternate verses from one side of a chapel to the other (this is the origin of Antiphonal Singing). The centre of each day is the celebration of the Eucharist, in a formalised pattern. This will include readings from the Old and New Testaments, an act of the confession of sins, prayers of intercession, and prayers of thanksgiving and praise. So after the hearing of God's word, the four main parts of Christian prayer – praise, thanksgiving, confession and intercession – are expressed. The heart of the Eucharist, however, is the remembrance and re-presentation of the self-offering of Christ, and sharing in the consecrated bread and wine, which is a sharing in the 'body and blood', the risen life, of Christ.

In the Eucharist, or the Mass, the community recalls the 'Last Supper' Jesus shared with his disciples before he went to his death. Then Jesus commanded the disciples to take, bless, break and eat bread, saying to them, 'This is my body'. Similarly, he commanded them to take, bless and drink wine, saying, 'This is my blood of the new covenant'. There have been various interpretations of this saying, but almost all Christians accept that taking wine and eating bread in memory of Jesus is a central part of the public prayer of the church.

Some Christians take these statements literally, and insist that Jesus' body and blood is really and truly present on the altar. The best known example is the Roman Catholic doctrine of transubstantiation, by which the 'substance' of bread and wine is said to change into the 'substance' of Jesus' body and blood, while the 'accidents' or visible qualities remain those of bread and wine. Other Christians, like the Eastern Orthodox, Anglicans and Lutherans, agree that Jesus is really and truly present on the altar, but do not define in what way this is so. The bread and wine are taken to be the means by which Jesus, in his risen life, is locally present among worshippers, because he wills it to be so. Other more Protestant Christians, while accepting that Jesus is present wherever disciples gather in his name, take this to be a spiritual presence only. Even then, however, the Lord's Supper is accepted as an especially solemn way of celebrating the presence of Christ among his people, which was indeed commanded by Jesus himself.

For Catholics, the Mass is a real propitiatory sacrifice, though it is not a new sacrifice. It makes present the one sacrifice that Jesus made by giving up his own life so that his Father's will could be done. This sacrifice also manifested the self-giving of the eternal Word of God for the sake of the world, and so it can be truly made present, or re-presented, on altars throughout the world. Some Protestants do not like talking of sacrifice, since this might tempt people into thinking that priests can do something new to influence God, that Jesus has not already done. They see the Lord's Supper more as a commemoration of Jesus' sacrifice on the Cross, which can never be repeated. Again, however, all Christians see this rite as a way commanded by Jesus in which his sacrifice, which is also the sacrifice of the eternal Word for the sake of all humanity, can be made vividly present to worshippers.

The final act of the Eucharist is the communion, when the worshippers eat the bread and drink the wine in memory of Jesus. Protestants stress this aspect of the rite more than any other, and accept it as a symbol, or even as a divinely appointed means, of receiving the spiritual life of Christ into their own lives. Catholics and the Orthodox also accept communion as an important part of the rite, but hold that it is not essential to take communion in order to participate in the rite. For them, it is enough on most occasions to adore Christ, as he is represented before them as giving his life for their salvation.

In the history of Christianity, there have been great arguments about these differing interpretations of the Eucharist, and some differences remain. But most Christians now accept that the important thing is to celebrate the rite, intending to do whatever Jesus commanded, so that the exact interpretation can be left open. At the time of writing, however, Roman Catholics still forbid communion together with Protestants, since they feel that the differences in interpretation – about the real presence and the sacrifice of the Mass – are too great for visible unity. Certainly, there are differences in the way the rite is celebrated in different churches. In Catholic churches, there is often great pomp and ceremony, and a daily celebration of the rite. In some Protestant churches, the Lord's Supper is a simple ceremony of sharing bread and wine, which is held perhaps once a month after a service of prayer. The reality underlying both, however, is still the self-giving sacrifice of the Eternal Word, manifested in the self-sacrifice of Jesus on the Cross, and made present again in the commemoration of that sacrifice in the Eucharist or Supper of the Lord.

The Holy Communion brings out a central feature of the Christian view of prayer – namely, that God comes to meet us before we seek for him, and that he unites us to himself by his own action of self-giving love. So public prayer is not primarily thought of as something we do. It is rather something that God does in and through us. That is why we can use standard and formalised words in the liturgy. We are participating in a ritual activity, by which we share in the adoration of God which all creation owes to its creator, the source and epitome of all its beauty and wisdom.

The church is the 'body of Christ', the material embodiment of the life of Christ, and so its public worship seeks to make this embodiment a reality. To help people share in the life of Christ, which is meant to transform their own lives into images of the eternal God, the church divides each year into fasts and festivals in which different aspects of the life of Jesus are commemorated. In the course of the Christian year, the faithful are invited to share in the communal repetition of the life of Christ. The church's year begins with Advent, in November, with a time of looking forward to the coming of Christ, the fulfilment of the promises of God. At the time of the winter solstice, in the darkest days of the year in the northern hemisphere, Christmas, the festival of the birth of Jesus, celebrates the coming of the light into a world of darkness, and the birth of Christ in human hearts. A month or so later, Holy Week and Good Friday complete the six-week fast of Lent, when the suffering and self-giving love of Christ is contemplated, and the faithful are invited to follow him in giving up their lives in the service of others.

Almost immediately, the festival of Easter celebrates the resurrection, the triumph of life which is stronger than all the powers of death and destruction. The festival usually coincides with the northern spring, when the world turns from the dark and cold of winter, and breaks into new life and vitality. Six weeks later, at Pentecost, the church recalls and re-enacts the coming of the Holy Spirit with power, the event with which the life of the church really began. And then, through the long green days of summer, the gospel accounts of the life of Jesus are retold, presenting the pattern which is that of all Christian lives, a pattern of forgiveness, healing, care for the poor, and patient compassion.

In this way, the church seeks to mould human lives on the pattern of love which it sees in Jesus, and which is shaped by the present action of the Holy Spirit. It seeks to invite people into a community which is called to be 'the body of Christ', forgiving, healing and bringing God near to those who are lost in sin, as Jesus did in Galilee. Many Protestant churches do not find the ceremonial and formal prayer of the church helpful. They stress the importance of informal and extempore prayer, and look for spontaneity and freshness of approach in public worship. Sometimes they even accuse the public liturgy of encouraging 'vain repetition' and useless ceremony. Most Protestants, however, would accept the usefulness of a disciplined reading of Scripture and a formal remembrance of Jesus' life, even if their own preference is for a more direct and individually creative approach.

## SECOND VIEW: DEVOTION

A more personal approach exists within both Catholic and Protestant traditions, though it is more characteristic of the Protestant in recent European history. Indeed, one source of the Protestant Reformation was a felt need for the expression of an intense personal devotion to Christ, which could be realised without the mediation of a priestly or institutional authority. Public liturgy tends to be rather formal and without overt expressions of emotion. What matters is that things are done in the correct way, and with due reverence and sobriety. If there is a personal impact, it happens more indirectly, as the inculcation of a mood or frame of mind which derives from the daily repetition of Scriptural material. Devotional prayer consists rather in the direct response of the heart to the personal impact of Jesus Christ. It is the response of the beloved to the one who has shown his great love by giving up his life, and who has sent his Spirit into the hearts of men and women to inspire them with joy and hope.

The earliest records of church meetings in the New Testament certainly speak of very informal meetings, when people would stand up to prophesy, or contribute a hymn or a prayer, and 'speaking in tongues' would occur, when people, filled with the Spirit, would speak without using the words of any known language, while others would apparently translate for the congregation (1 Corinthians 14:26–33). This phenomenon, of being filled with the Spirit, is characteristic of Pentecostal or charismatic churches, where a vibrant and emotional tone is sustained by regular experiences of the Spirit, inspiring new and strange forms of utterance. The experience of the disciples at the feast of Pentecost, in Jerusalem (Acts 2:1–4), seems to have been of this sort. The apostles spoke in ways which each person heard 'in their own language' – a phenomenon very like that of speaking in tongues, a speech which is translated into a natural language by others who are present.

Such ecstatic prayer is attributed to the activity of the Holy Spirit, and St Paul is careful to say that its chief point is to increase the fruits of joy, peace, patience and love in the lives of disciples. It is not to demonstrate any sort of spiritual superiority, but to give a lively sense of the presence and power of God in one's own life.

Such prayer is devotional, for it consists almost entirely in praising God for his goodness and thanking God for his mighty acts of salvation, for his forgiveness of human sin, and his gift of new life in Jesus. Of course intercession – asking for things – is part of prayer, since one would naturally ask help from anyone with whom one had a deep personal relationship. But praise and thanksgiving are the chief parts of devotional prayer, since what it does is to give expression to the thankful love and reverent adoration which arises when one contemplates the creator and redeemer of all things.

Devotion is naturally centred on God, but for Christians it is centred on the personal form of God, on God as enfleshed in human history, and therefore on the person of Jesus. God in his aspect as the creator of the cosmos may rightly be thought of as too sublime and terrible for any sort of personal relationship with humans to be possible. But if Jesus truly showed what God is, in a human and approachable form, then we can relate to Jesus in a straightforwardly human way, as his disciples did. And in so relating, we do truly relate to God, even if it is to God only insofar as God can be truly expressed in human form.

In relating to Jesus as the Saviour, the one who takes human form in order to liberate humanity from the consequences of selfish desire, we are also able to relate to the uncreated source of all as 'Father'. God the creator takes on personal form, but only when regarded as the father of Jesus, as the one who graciously becomes a father to humans because he has, in one aspect ('the Word or Son') taken human form.

God is seen thus for the sake of limited and finite persons. In his eternal and glorious nature, the Word of God is infinite, and as awesome as is God the ungenerated creator. Yet that Word is truly expressed in Jesus, and though the glorified form of Jesus is probably very different from anything we can imagine, still he continues to relate to us, as he related to the disciples after his raising from death, in human form. So there is a proper form of Christian prayer in which we can talk to Jesus as friend and brother, as the one who suffered death for us, and who reigns in glory as our spiritual King.

Personal devotion to Jesus can take many forms, from the adoration of the infant in the cradle or in his mother's arms, to the contemplation of him calling little children to himself, or showing his sacred heart of love, to the crucified figure who gives himself for us, and to the King who reigns at the right hand of the Father. All these images are ways of making the humanity of God real to us, and of calling forth in us an emotional response of delight and love.

Christian devotion may seem simple and unaffected, and it has the power to move the simplest heart, in its presentation of Jesus as a person who evokes our gratitude, loyalty and joy. Yet it is in fact of the deepest complexity. The Jesus whose friendship Christians claim is the human face of that cosmic wisdom on whom the stars themselves are patterned, and in whom the whole universe will ultimately be united. The love with which we love him is placed within the heart by the action of the Holy Spirit, who utters terms of love beyond any human power of speech. And affectionate love of Jesus passes imperceptibly into a sense of complete dependence upon that ungenerated source of all things, the Father of the eternal Son, upon whom we utterly depend at every moment, and without whom we would completely cease to be.

The love of Jesus is no superficial emotion, and yet it is a way in which God makes himself available even, or especially, to those with the innocence of children. In the hymns of the Wesleys, founders of Methodism; in the ecstatic utterances of Pentecostal assemblies; and in the quiet Catholic devotion to the Sacred Heart of Jesus, God is made known as a genuinely personal presence, the one whose love is stronger than death, and who wills to enfold us in his love for ever.

## THIRD VIEW: CONTEMPLATION

If prayer is the conscious relating of mind and heart to God, then its nature will differ according to the way this relationship is conceived. Some people conceive of God as a Ruler to whom one relates as an obedient servant. One might think of this as a first stage of relationship, open to all who have a sense of a personal creator.

Christians usually think of God as Father, adopting a relationship of child to parent. This is possible insofar as Christians live 'in Christ', and so share in the intimate form of relationship Jesus had to the one he called 'Abba', father. Of course, God can be regarded as 'Mother' too, as Mother Julian of Norwich did, since God surely embodies whatever good and loving attributes we might attribute to parents of different sexes. This second stage of human–divine relationship is one in which God enables us to relate to the divine in a more personal, intimate way.

The heart of the Christian gospel is that 'God is love', and so there is a third stage of relationship, that of the lover to the beloved. At this stage prayer becomes, at its best, a wordless union of love, in which the human mind is suffused with a sense of divine goodness, and may achieve an ecstasy of joy in union with a personal being of infinite love.

Most of those who are called 'mystics' in the Christian tradition experience and write of this third stage, and of the way to it. The twelfth-century saint Bernard of Clairvaux used the imagery of the Song of Songs to speak of the soul as a bride who longs to consummate marital union with the spiritual bridegroom. In the sixteenth century, Teresa of Avila describes the experience of 'divine marriage' when God in rapture unites the soul with himself. The mystical experience is a state of the soul when it is taken beyond itself into a union with God that is described as like marital bliss. To experience this is the greatest possible state of happiness for humans, and in such experience prayer is simply delight in union with God.

John of the Cross warns, however, that blissful experience is not what the prayer of union aims at. Prayer must simply aim at God for God's own sake, for the sheer beauty and glory of the divine being. One may have to pass through the 'dark night of the soul' as a way of purifying one's egoistic desires, and the ascent to the vision of divine beauty may be long and arduous. Some Christians even suspect this path of prayer, because it seems to put such stress on

personal effort, on fasting and penance, on renunciation and sub-
jective experience. But Christian mystics stress that it is only God's
grace which can bring us to a sense of union. Fasting and medita-
tion are themselves consequences of God's initiating grace, and
they dispose the mind to a fuller sense of God's presence. Such
prayer is not selfish, because it motivates one to works of charity
and mercy, to share the life of God with others, not just to having
delightful inner sensations.

In Christian tradition there is a stage even beyond this experience
of bridal ecstasy. It is found in the influential works of Dionysius
(probably a fifth-century Syrian monk) and in the fourteenth-century
anonymous work, *The Cloud of Unknowing*, as well as in Meister
Eckhart, the thirteenth-century Dominican. At this stage, all sense of
individual selfhood is lost, and one passes silently, as Dionysius puts
it, 'to the ineffable and transcendent God beyond all speech and
thought'. In this cloud of unknowing, there is only 'a dark gazing into
the simple being of God himself alone'. It is even said that all sensa-
tion and thought is abandoned, in a unity 'with the beyond being and
knowing', an ultimate non-duality of which nothing can be said,
though the way to it can be obscurely indicated.

The third and fourth stages comprise, in Christian tradition, the
way of contemplation, the prayer of quiet in which one seeks, not to
speak and not even imaginatively to call up scenes from the life of
Christ, but simply to enter into the divine presence. Probably the
models of loving relationship and of wordless union need to be held
together, as one merges into the other, and neither is complete without some trace of the other. But in these forms of contemplative
prayer, both formal liturgy and the public expression of deep emotion are transcended, as the individual soul finds its being at once
fulfilled and transcended into absorption into the life of God. It is in
all these forms of prayer, however, that one finds the heart and driv-
ing force which makes Christianity a living and dynamic faith.

# 16 ETERNAL LIFE

C hristian faith is not primarily about life after death. It is about living in conscious loving relationship to God now. 'Eternal life' is primarily life lived in relation to the eternal, not life going on for ever. Nevertheless, most Christians are committed to believing that there is a form of existence for humans after their bodily death. This is not least because the Christian faith is based largely on the apostles' claim to have seen Jesus alive, in a new and glorious form, after his bodily death. But it is also based on the thought that a God of universal love would not let millions of human lives end in suffering and frustration, without attaining to any knowledge of God, and without enjoying the good things that creation offers. Even those who do have some experience of God in their lives would wish for a fuller and more intense knowledge and love of God than this life usually seems to offer.

Christians believe that God will take all the good things of creation into the divine experience, eliminating the evil and enjoying the good. It then seems that, if God could give creatures a fuller share in the divine experience of created values, by giving persons some form of existence after their bodily deaths, it would be a positively good thing to do. Believers in God therefore have good reason to hope for a post-death existence, in which they can love God more fully, realise some of the possibilities of their lives which were tragically frustrated by circumstances, and share in some appropriate way God's experience of the created cosmos.

The good news that God raised Jesus from death so that human beings could share the divine life is an important part of Christian faith. The general outlines of Christian belief about human existence after death are fairly clear, but there are different ways of interpreting them. The various interpretations differ largely according to how literal, metaphorical or symbolic the Biblical language about these things is taken to be.

## FIRST VIEW: A LITERAL INTERPRETATION

One interpretation takes the Biblical language as literally as possible. At some time in the future of the planet earth, Jesus – who now exists in a glorified form in the presence of God – will return to the earth with the angelic host to fight against Satan and the forces of evil, who are now freely roaming the planet. There may be a period in which he will rule for 1000 years. But there will eventually be a decisive conflict in which the Devil will be overthrown, and which will issue in the Day of Judgement.

At the Day of Judgement, all the dead will rise from their graves, in bodies which have been resurrected by God, and will face the judgement of God on their deeds. The evil will be cast into the fires of Hell, where they will exist for ever in torment. The good, or those who have faith in Christ, will be members of a newly refashioned Heaven and earth, where there is no sea and where it is always day, and there they will live for ever in the joy of the presence of God.

This is the Protestant version of a literalist interpretation of the Bible. The Catholic version is rather different. When humans die, Catholics believe that the human soul, which is the subject of responsible action and intellectual understanding, continues to exist without the body. The souls of saints enter Heaven, the presence of God, and there they can continue to pray for those still on earth. In Roman Catholic doctrine, Mary the mother of Jesus has already been assumed, body and soul, into Heaven, and so is now in the state in which all the faithful hope eventually to be. Mary, as the mother of God, has a special place in Christian devotion, not as divine, but as a soul filled with grace by her divine son, and therefore a model of virtue and faith. In Catholic devotion, she is regarded as having been crowned Queen of Heaven. She cannot be worshipped, but she can properly be revered as the greatest of all the saints who are united to God by grace. Devotion to Mary is one of the most characteristic marks of the Roman Catholic and Eastern Orthodox churches, and many miraculous apparitions of Mary have been claimed all over the world. Nevertheless, it is as mother of Jesus that she is revered, and as being the divinely chosen vehicle of the Incarnation of the eternal Son of God.

The souls of the wicked enter into Hell. But the souls of the faithful, which are as yet too imperfect to enter directly into the presence of God, enter an intermediate state, Purgatory. There they suffer pains of purgation, where the last traces of sin are burned from them, and where they are comforted by the assurance of final salvation. The prayers of the faithful on earth can help the plight of those in Purgatory, and the church can give Indulgences, in response to the prayers or penitential practices of the faithful, which will remit some of their punishment.

When the history of earth has run its course, and when the holy souls in Purgatory have completed the process of purification, Christ will return to the earth, and the Day of Judgement will follow. All the dead will receive back their bodies, and in those resurrected bodies the final judgement will be given on their ultimate destination – the presence of God or the torment of separation from God for ever.

What is common to these literalist interpretations is that all human beings will be resurrected and judged according to what they have done during their earthly lives. It may be that the inevitable penalty of life without faith is eternal torment, because no human being can escape the guilt of original sin, or live a life of perfect goodness. Christ, however, saves all those who turn to him in faith (or, perhaps, in implicit faith), and he himself pays the penalty that would have been theirs. By the grace of God expressed in Christ, then, many people are received into eternal life for ever, who in fact deserved only death. That is the ultimate hope and assurance that Christian faith offers – salvation from the torments of Hell, and life with God for ever. Such things are to be found painted on the walls of many medieval churches, and they have shaped the Christian imagination for many centuries.

## SECOND VIEW: A METAPHORICAL INTERPRETATION

For many Christians, the medieval paintings show precisely what the status of Biblical language about life after death is – it is a series of pictures or metaphorical images whose primary function is to shape the Christian imagination. It was never meant to be taken literally. When Jesus spoke in parables, he was telling stories whose point was to evoke a particular moral or spiritual insight. When he used striking aphorisms (about camels going through the eyes of needles, for example), he was using exaggerated images to reinforce a teaching in a memorable way. So, when the Bible speaks of the battle with Satan, of the return of Christ in glory, of the fires of Gehenna which will never be quenched, and of angels singing around the throne of God, these are memorable images to express spiritual truths, not literal descriptions of future events.

Even the stories of Jesus' resurrection are not to be taken as literal accounts. They vividly portray the apostles' sense that Jesus had conquered death, and was somehow present with them. They speak of the triumph of love over death, of the possibility of new life even in the worst circumstances, and of a transformation of human life by a self-sacrificial obedience to God. So the resurrection is not the revival of a corpse. It is new life with God, obtained by taking up one's cross to follow Jesus, by dying to all that holds one back from the love of God.

When the Bible speaks of a battle with Satan, and of the *parousia*, the making-present, of Christ, it is not talking about some future historical battle, or about the arrival of some physical body on a cloud. It is talking about the inner war between love and hatred, between goodness and selfish desire, which marks all of human history. And it is proclaiming that the goal (the 'end') of human history is the emergence of a truly human community, in which peace and justice will flourish, in which evil and suffering will be finally overcome, and in which the whole human community will become the 'body' or presence of Christ in the physical cosmos.

For such a metaphorical interpretation of Biblical language, talk about the Day of Judgement is not referring to an actual time in the future. It represents the fact that people stand before God at every moment of time, to be judged on their response to God's challenge to renounce selfish desire and turn to the power of love. Just as the Creation is not a first moment in time, but is the dependence of every time on God, so the Last Judgement is not a last moment in time, but is the relation of every time to God, in faith or in unbelief, in obedience or in rejection.

When people reject God, they are rejecting the obligation to serve the needs of others. They thereby place themselves outside the realm of love, in an 'outer darkness' where they are, in their deepest selves, solitary and loveless. One can speak of them as destroyed by the flames of their own desires. The flames of the rubbish-heap (the Bible never speaks of 'Hell', but uses a number of different images to portray human life without God) are the self-destroying flames of selfish desire. The person who rejects God chooses the way of death, for there is ultimately no life without God, who is its only sustainer.

On the other hand, when people accept God, when they confess their sin and failure and rely on the loving kindness of God alone, then their lives are opened up to a power of love greater than their own. The giving up of self to God is the entrance into eternal life, life which is transfigured by its union with the eternal reality of God. Biblical talk of paradise and of the outer darkness or the flames of the rubbish-heap places before humans the two ways, of self-destructive death or God-centred life, which lie before them at every moment of their lives.

For some Christians, one can use this language without any thought of a literal life after death at all. It is all a matter of placing before people the decisive choice between good and evil, with its consequences for self-destruction or self-transcendence. To introduce thoughts of an existence after death would, they think, distract attention from the real point of the imagery, which is to challenge one to a decision between spiritual life and death in the midst of historical time.

For others, the Christian faith does maintain that there is a form of human existence which transcends earthly life, a life beyond time. But, precisely because it is beyond time, it can only be spoken of in inadequate images. Beyond death, each human life is taken up into the eternal timelessness of God, and there all that has been done in earthly life, for good and ill, is in some way seen and experienced for what it is. There is a Judgement, a Heaven and a Hell. But what these images represent is an eternal state in which each person finds their life either accepted into the eternal reality of the divine life or excluded from it.

Christians speak of the resurrection of the body and the communion of saints in order to stress that it is the whole person, not just some disembodied soul, which is taken into the eternal life of God. And this eternal life is not a solitary life. It is more a matter of communion, a timeless fellowship with other created persons and with God, which is somehow the fulfilment of all the fragmentary and fleeting moments of life in history.

If eternal life really is eternal (that is, timeless), we cannot properly comprehend it while we are in time. Yet the Christian might still hope for eternal life, hoping that each moment of this life will be timelessly related to God in a positive way, beyond the disadvantages of time, which brings decay and forgetfulness with it, and held for ever in the mind of God.

On such a view, talk in the Catholic tradition of Purgatory, of the intercession of the saints, and of prayers and Masses for the dead, may seem particularly hard to interpret. But some Catholic theologians, like Karl Rahner for instance, have construed such talk as concerned with holding the dead in mind as one prays to God, and with having a sense of the eternal communion between living and dead in God.

The image of Purgatory might be associated with a non-temporal idea of degrees of purification, so that each person is eternally related to God in a unique way, depending on the degree of their own faith, while being assured of unbreakable union with God.

## THIRD VIEW: A REALIST AND NON-LITERAL INTERPRETATION

If one has a view of God as a uniquely eternal being, of whom one can only speak in analogy and metaphor, then it may indeed seem that speaking of the relation of the whole of an earthly life to the eternal God may also be properly construed in terms of analogy and metaphor. The metaphorical interpretation of Biblical talk of life after death insists on this fact, and on the fact that any talk of eternal life must ultimately be taken in a non-temporal sense. However, many Christians hold that talk of life after death cannot all be metaphorical. At some point the metaphors must stand for some sort of literal state-ment. So a third interpretation of Biblical language is possible, accord-ing to which it is largely metaphorical, but has a factual basis which can, at least to some extent, be disentangled from the metaphors and which does point to some literal expectations about the future, and about a continued personal existence after bodily death.

One important starting point for such an interpretation is the New Testament accounts of the resurrection of Jesus. There is no doubt that the apostles claimed to have seen Jesus after his bodily death, but the manner of his appearing is mysterious. He left the tomb, according to Matthew's gospel, even though the entrance was still blocked by a large stone. He was often unrecognised – even on a seven-mile walk to Emmaus – he appeared to them behind locked doors, he appeared for short periods and suddenly disappeared again, and finally he 'ascended into heaven'. That is, he disappeared from the physical universe altogether, being taken to the presence of the Father.

Paul claimed to have seen the risen Lord on the road to Damascus, but what he experienced was a blinding light and a voice. So the form in which Jesus appeared was no ordinary material body. In the central New Testament passage on the resurrection – the first letter to the Corinthians, chapter fifteen – Paul stresses that the resurrection body is quite unlike the material body. He writes that it will not decay, it will not be 'flesh and blood', and it will be a 'spiritual body', not a materially embodied soul.

The obvious implication is that Jesus continued to exist after bodily death, but no longer in a material body. He existed in another realm, not anywhere in the physical universe, and he was able to appear from time to time to his disciples in a fully material form, for a period of about six weeks. After that, he ceased appearing in this universe, but continued to exist in union with God, and on a different plane of being.

Many of the first Christians believed that Jesus would return to this universe in a short time, bringing evil and injustice to an end, and ushering in the Messianic kingdom of peace. But there are contrasting strands of thought in the New Testament. It quickly came to be accepted that the gospel of eternal life through Jesus was to be preached throughout the whole world – which would take quite a long time. Moreover, the church was to be the body of Christ, carrying out his work of healing and reconciling – so the church has a positive role to play, which would be frustrated if the world came to a sudden end. And there is an important line of thought (in the letters to the Colossians and Ephesians, for example) for which all things 'in heaven and on earth' are to be united in Christ – which implies a long period of development and spiritual growth for the cosmos.

All this suggests to many that these are metaphors for the underlying expectation that one day, late or soon, evil will be obliterated from creation, the liberation of humanity from death and corruption will be complete, and the cosmic Christ who was known in the life of Jesus will be manifested in a new and glorious form. We do not know whether this will happen within this universe as it now is, or whether it will happen after the billion-year history of this universe has come to an end, when a new universe will come into being.

The New Testament imagery seems to speak partly in a symbolic way of historical events – of the coming of Christ in the church, gathering people from the corners of the earth into a community of a new covenant (so one could interpret the symbolic imagery of Christ coming on the clouds with angels, and the gathering of the elect from all the earth). And it seems to speak partly of the ultimate manifestation of Christ at the end of historical time, when all those who have ever lived will undergo a final judgement on all that their lives have been. These two thoughts are poetically blended together, so that we can see the challenge and invitation of Christ in our present lives as a making-present of the ultimate future in which all things will be judged in the presence of Christ. In that sense, we can think of Christ as coming at each moment, unexpectedly, like a 'thief in the night', because each moment will be seen for what it truly is when Christ is fully present in glory.

The final judgement will come with the full manifestation of the Christ in glory, and it will involve the resurrection of all those personal and responsible agents who have ever existed in this universe. We might think of the 'Last Judgement' as the final statement of how created persons stand before God, in the ultimate choices for good and evil which were realised in their earthly lives. It is possible that, in their freedom and pride, some may refuse to accept the love of God, if its price is the renunciation of selfish desire. In that case, they will receive an 'eternal punishment'. This will not, however, be unending torture, which seems incompatible with the loving-kindness of God. It will be final separation from God, a punishment in the eyes of all who know and love God. Most people who take this interpretation believe that at that point such miserable souls will be annihilated. Being beyond repentance and without joy, they will cease to exist, perhaps simply disintegrating into bundles of incoherent and conflicting desires which finally burn themselves away. They will certainly not be members of the resurrection world, in which 'there shall no more be anything accursed' (Revelation 22:3).

Those who have overcome self and have received the divine love, will enter into the new creation which is the world of the resurrection, where there exist literally unending joys and possibilities of creating and enjoying new values and activities, in full awareness of the presence of a God of infinite perfection. The Christian gospel is clear that such a life, eternal life, is not confined to those who have been morally good in their earthly lives. The whole point of God's self-manifestation in Jesus is to show that God forgives all sin, on condition only of repentance, contrition and an effort to make amends by depending on the mercy of God. Salvation is by faith, not works, which means that all who sincerely turn to God will be brought into the divine presence for ever.

The Christian hope is not that we will then exist in the very same material bodies that we have now. It is that persons will exist, like Jesus, in spiritual bodies, and in quite a different form of being. The New Testament speaks of the creation of a 'new heaven and earth', a new form of existence altogether, where there is no evil or destruction, and therefore where the laws of nature themselves are entirely different. Modern physics tells us that the planet earth will come to an end. It will eventually be swallowed up by the sun. In time the whole universe will come to an end, as the law of entropy eventually causes everything to run out of energy. For Christian faith, there will be an end of everything in this universe, yet human life will not end. It will continue in a new creation, when all those who have been redeemed by Christ will exist in a more glorious and blissful form, in the presence of God for ever.

Particular images of the resurrection are metaphors for something we cannot literally imagine. The literal truth behind the metaphors, for this sort of interpretation, is that we will continue to exist in different forms of embodiment, in which we can act, share experiences, and relate to one another in new and exciting ways. The 'resurrection of the body' is the existence of human beings, in fully creative and communal ways, in this richer and more wonderful form of life, and in full consciousness of the presence of God.

It seems obvious, however, that most of us are not yet ready for such a life in a perfect creation, and that when we die, we will not be prepared to face such a final judgement on our lives. We may never have heard of God's promise of redemptive love. We may not have realised the seriousness and destructiveness of our greed and hatred. We may not be free of the power and consequences of sin. Even after bodily death, we need to be prepared for the final judgement on our lives.

So there are images in the Bible of an intermediate state where there exists both punishment for sin and the possibility of a development towards more loving and integrated personalities. These images develop the ancient Hebrew idea of Sheol, the world of shadows, into the idea of a realm in which people come to realise the harm they have done by their deeds, and experience in themselves the suffering they have caused to others. Images also exist in the New Testament of Paradise, a realm of cool water and beautiful trees and meadows, where one can rejoice in the presence of the Patriarchs and prophets, and where one might still go on learning more about God and the divine purpose.

Obviously, no one has the details of such an intermediate existence (though that is the realm to which Jesus is said to have 'descended' after his death). But the basic idea behind it is that, in a morally ordered universe, those who have done evil must suffer in themselves what they have inflicted on others, and those who have been faithful and virtuous should find a happiness that may have been denied them on earth. Presumably also, if the Christian belief is true, those who have not known Christ on earth will learn the real nature of God and his redeeming work in Christ.

This intermediate stage cannot be called the resurrection world, for it is not a world of perfection and peace. In it we might imagine the dead as embodied in ways which are appropriate to the working-out of the desires and ambitions which they formulated on earth. Eventually, all created persons will have had sufficient opportunity to turn from evil and to learn enough of God to be able to receive the divine love in a full and unmediated way. Only then will they be ready to face the final judgement.

In that final judgement, however, will there still be a great division between those who enter into the love of God, and those who stand condemned by their refusal to accept it, even after every opportunity has been given to them? We may be sure that 'The Lord is forbearing, not wishing that any shall perish, but that all should reach repentance' (2 Peter 3:9). God certainly wishes all created persons to be saved. Indeed, there are strong hints in the New Testament that all might be saved, and live in the knowledge and love of God. The first letter to the Corinthians says that 'as in Adam all die, so shall all be made alive' (1 Corinthians 15:22). And the letter to the Romans says that 'God has consigned all men to disobedience, that he may have mercy upon all' (Romans 11:32).

It may be better to be cautious, however, and say only that the God revealed in Christ desires all created persons to be saved, and so will make it possible for all to be saved. Yet it may well seem that a loving God would not allow anyone to continue an existence in misery for ever, so the idea of an everlasting Hell should be renounced, as a misinterpretation of the gospel sayings about the gravity and destructiveness of sin. What awaits any who finally reject God is final destruction.

The idea of an everlasting life with God, on the other hand, seems deeply consistent with the idea of a God who wills to share awareness of good things with others, and whose reality, being infinite, offers absolutely limitless good things to be shared. So we might think of eternal life as a continuing temporal life, in which there are always new things to be learned and enjoyed, in which there is never any sense of tedium or boring repetition, and in which the whole of existence is transformed by the clearly apprehended love of God. The hope for such an everlasting life is a natural extension of the hope for clearer knowledge and love of God, and so it might be seen as an implication of the present awareness of the love of God which Christian faith aims to evoke.

These three interpretations of life after death are very different, but they share the belief that the good and evil we do in this life is of eternal significance, that God offers eternal life to all who turn to him in faith, and that the ending of life, and of the universe itself, does not undermine the Christian hope for an eternal life with God which transcends earthly existence. The purpose of the creator God is to offer eternal life to all who are willing to accept the free offer of the divine love, manifested in Jesus the Christ, and made present to us by the divine Spirit. The creator's purpose is to unite our lives for ever to the eternal life of God.

◆

Different understandings of Christian faith are different ways of trying to work out what this basic gospel implies. But the gospel itself, Christians would say, rests on the revelation, the self-disclosure, of the being and purpose of God in the life and death of Jesus, and on the experience of his risen presence in the fellowship of disciples. The Christian faith has many interpretations, and many different forms of existence, but underneath all its often seemingly complex and disputed doctrines it has a fundamental simplicity.

Its root is the disclosure of the nature of God as love, in the events surrounding Jesus. Its goal is the uniting of human lives to the life of God. And the way to that goal is sharing in the power of the Spirit of God, who transforms temporal lives into images and vehicles of eternal love. Some Christians would want to add other elements as of fundamental importance, but I think all would agree that at least these three things are at the core of Christianity. This short introduction has tried to indicate some of the ways in which Christian thinkers through the ages have tried to spell out different elaborations of this core in different ages and times. The process of interpretation is by no means at an end, and Christian faith will no doubt go on growing and changing in response to new insights and situations. But it will never abandon its primary witness to the disclosure of the nature and purpose of God for humanity, which is held to have occurred around the life of that challenging and unforgettable human being, Jesus of Nazareth.

# INDEX